Tea Tips

A Guide to Enjoying Tea

Choose it to meet your tastes
Buy it to get value
Brew it to make it flavorful and fresh
Explore it to open up new choices

Peter G.W. Keen

Keen, Peter G.W.

Tea Tips: A Guide to Enjoying Tea

For Sherry, for always

ISBN-13: 978-1505788044
ISBN-10: 1505788048

Subjects: 1. Tea. 2. Tea industry. 3. Tea buying
Published in the United States

Table of Contents

Acknowledgements

A book doesn't emerge by just tapping fingers on keyboards. There's some truth in the image of the lonely writer laboring away in solitary shadows, looking for the words, editing and reediting, and doing it all again. And again. But writing is made productive and enjoyable by a network of help. Here are members of mine, to whom I express my warm appreciation and thanks.

First, to Rohan Jahargirdar who gave me a forum for my writing when he was director of marketing for Teabox. Rohan helped me achieve my unique if inconsequential niche as the globe's only known Singapore-born, British-native, US-resident, Indian-publication tea journalist. I've benefited, too, from Gopal Baskita Upadhayay's expertise in pointing me to interesting new teas.

Aravinda Anantharaman has been a wonderful support and I cannot thank her enough for all her collegiality and superb professional skills. Aravinda is the Senior Editor and publisher of Still Steeping, the tea blog she built up, now ranked in the top five in the world. She encouraged me to expand the scope of my tea writing and research and created a terrific showcase for a pool of writers and experts to explore history, lifestyle, industry and educational aspects of tea. She also has a patience and consideration people like me don't deserve but do value.

My family contributed in so many ways to *Tea Tips*. My daughter Sara helped me immeasurably in structuring, brainstorming and editing, and took many of the photographs. She has also become my second opinion tea-tester. Sherry, my wife, has been through all this before and makes the path smooth and warm, tolerating the tins, packets, pots cups and paper that comprise my "testing" of teas.

Bill Richardson has been a generous encourager of my work and linked me to his friends who have been equally generous in their gifts to me of several rare teas not available in the US. Thank you, to Lucy Han and to the memory of David Chen for their thoughtfulness. And to Karen Kennedy, for both friendship and that lovely gongfu travelling tea set.

So... It's done! Done!! Thanks, guys, for everything.

Preface: About *Tea Tips*

Tea Tips is not a book "*about*" teas but a guide to help you enjoy as wide a range of them as you feel it's worth your knowing about, and to get best value in your purchases. There's far more to choose from than you'll find on the shelves of supermarkets and the typical tea bag is as representative of the 3,000 teas on the market as instant coffee is of mochas, lattes and cappuccinos, or as hot dogs are of steak.

At the same time, there's no reason to fall for the hype and snobbery about tea and end up paying a premium for the packaging and Royal names. Even the best is relatively inexpensive, except for a few rare and specially crafted ones: typically, less than 50 cents a cup for a tea with a combination of flavors and aromas as varied as those among wines.

The goal of *Tea Tips* is to give you a sense of the choices and how to pick the ones for you. *Tea Tips* is just a navigation aid: a map of the territory with suggestions on where to stop, side trips and special sights. You don't have to become an expert or tea snob to find them. But you won't know what you'd like if you don't know what's out there. That goes well beyond the tea bag.

Tea is marked by two very distinct paths from the bush where the fresh leaf grows to the finished leaf that ends up in your cup: Artisan and Agribusiness. The question *Tea Tips* aims at answering is What is it worth *your* knowing about this?

> *How tea is made*, what creates the differences and what to look for. It's all about the leaf. Artisan whole leaf tea relies on hand plucking at seasonal peaks to select the "two buds and a leaf" that contain hundreds of compounds that the processing brings out, combines or suppresses to generate flavors, aromas, fullness, sweetness and layers of the tea "experience."
>
> Agribusiness tea farming uses machines, additives in many instances, advantages of scale, and streamlined production to make teas that are standardized and far less complex. Most of this is broken leaf and tea dust.

Myths and misinformation that put people off tea or lull them into sticking with second-rate ones at top prices. Here are just two: (1) Green tea is lower in caffeine than black ones; on average, yes, but that's about as useful a piece of information as knowing that the average size of a bathroom in a US house is 40 square feet. There's no real difference among the teas. (2) English tea is special. There's no such thing, Earl Grey had nothing to do with the tea that carries his name and the top one is made in Poland. Dubai is the global hub for English tea bagging.

The complex issues of tea and health and weight loss: A whole industry has been built on hyping the wonders of tea but the scientific evidence is highly inconclusive. It doesn't cure illnesses, directly help you lose weight or prevent cancer, diabetes, tooth decay, etc.

Some "healthy' teas are downright scary, especially herbal ones and supplements. Too many of them are also dreadful; Korean powder tasting like it's been marinated in creosote.

Tea seems correlative with health but not causative. Choose the tea you enjoy; if it does indeed provide medicinal or lifestyle benefits, you'll get them anyway. Without grimacing.

Making tea: If you find tea too bitter or flat, it's more likely to be you than the tea: brewing it too long, at the wrong temperature or in the microwave. Look after the water and the tea will look after itself.

Shopping: Tea is not expensive. $80 for a pound sounds costly but it's 40 cents for a cup. Branded tea bags and blends are typically 20 cents a cup. About 80% of Artisan whole leaf ones are in the 20-50 cent range.

Where to shop is as important as what to buy. The supermarket shelf has lots of packages but they are mostly marketing variations on a narrow range of names and types – English Breakfast, Assam blend, etc. Specialty stores are as much to browse in as to spend money in. Boutique palaces offer great ambience, accessories and packaging, but at about double what you can buy the tea for online.

Just about every tea on the world market can be found online. You do need caution and a little knowledge. There are bargains and ripoffs. One of aims in *Tea Tips* is to help you sort out information and misinformation, hype and reality and zero in on the many terrific buys.

Exploring the wide range of options easily and inexpensively: If you prefer strong black teas, there are malty Assams and Ceylons, plus lighter and more aromatic Darjeelings and China Keemuns. If you like tea but dislike green ones, expand your space of choices and it's pretty certain that you will become an enthusiast, maybe of the Japanese teas that are as unusual, subtle and varied as its cuisine, or the scented Chinese jasmine infusions that are free of any bitterness or watery vegetal flavor. You are likely to discover Silver Needle and Moonlight white teas that are the peak of the craft.

It's your choice. I hope that you enjoy *Tea Tips* but more importantly that it helps you enjoy your tea by giving you practical briefings on those choices.

Choice and variety: Beyond the tea bag

It's all about the leaf

Tea Tips might more jazzily be subtitled *Terrific Teas for Less Than Fifty Cents a Cup*. It's a guide to enjoying whole leaf tea: how to *choose* it, *buy* it, *brew* it, and *explore* its many features and options. You have plenty to pick from. It's estimated that there are over 3,000 varieties on the market.

Here are just a few that are easy to shop for. They are very different in taste and flavor. They don't cost much – a few cents more than an Earl Grey tea bag and less than a cup of good coffee brewed at home.

Whole leaf teas, all from the same bush, all different due to how they are processed. No additives, chemicals. Only withering, rolling, heating and drying.

These teas include black, green, puehr and white teas from India, China, Japan, Taiwan, Nepal and Sri Lanka. But all are variants of the same Artisan craft of production that begins by plucking the most tender buds and leaves from the tip of the same *camellia sinensis* bush. These are nursed through a varying sequence of steps that form them to bring out a particular taste experience. This is all done without chemicals or additives.

The range of tastes across the teas is very much a set of themes and variations. Those of each style share a dominant flavor; this is the theme. Black tea is rich and robust and very distinct from the smooth lightness of greens, for instance. There are multiple variations; blacks may be malty, sharp, smoky or flowery.

The tea industry is divided into providers that build their offers very much around the themes, with Earl Grey and English Breakfast dominant examples. These are generic. Buyers know what they will taste like and expect consistency, with the differences being a little – a little lighter, a little sweeter, and of course a little cheaper.

Other tea producers focus on the variations. It's the littles that appeal and the differences that build reputation. Those multiply very quickly. The teas shown below, for instance, are all Japanese green teas – theme – but entirely different in flavor – variations. In a Japanese restaurant, you are likely to be proffered a bag in a cup of "green tea" or you can order a sencha. Which would you like... Uji, Asamushi, Shizuoka, Karigani? Maybe a Hachijuhachiya, where the distinctive taste comes from its being made 88 days after the start of the spring rains, versus shincha, the first-picked sencha of the year?

Japanese green teas: sencha, bancha, matcha, houjicha, kukicha, genmaicha.
Meticulous choice of which part of the leaf to use; sun-grown, shaded; steaming, roasting

What's the difference between these? Well, the average restaurant Japanese green teabag is a compelling reason to drink coffee. At best, it's bland. You drink it because it's there; it's not something you'd seek out. You don't have any idea of better choices and are wary about paying for something weird and costly. So, mediocre green it is, by default, not preference. You don't know what you don't know about the options.

If you apply the example to coffee or wine, rather than tea, the contrast is clear. People ordering them generally have a sense of the basics but that's not the case for tea. Most, for instance, assume that black and green teas come from different plants. They are unaware that buying a tea bag because it's an Earl Grey can be like paying a high price for a "vintage" boxed California-style Chardonnay (product of Baja, Mexico and a real product, not fictional).

You don't have to be an expert on wines to enjoy them but it helps to know some basics and be aware of choices – California Cabs versus Zinfs, for instance, or good years for Bordeaux. What should you pay for a decent Riesling? Is that $12 Chianti in a straw basket a bargain or expensively packaged mouthwash?

"Green tea" or "English Breakfast" is like "vin ordinaire" or "house red", and occasionally Baja Chardonnay. You can do better. Artisan crafted whole leaf teas give you extensive choices, with the equivalent of regional wine names, chateau estates, vintages. There's snobbery, too, neatly captured for wines in a cartoon as "It's just a naïve domestic Burgundy, but I think you'll be amused its presumption."

Teas are similarly identified by some name, category and source. These range from the useless – "Japanese tea", "blend of black teas", "Royal English Afternoon Palace Tea" – to the informative, such as "Darjeeling Seeyok (the estate name), First flush (Spring harvest), TGFOP (tippy golden flowery leaf grade)" or "Kagoshima kabuse sencha" (Region in Japan, cover-shaded growing, high grade leaf).

Informative descriptors point to what distinguishes a tea (Seeyok first flush), the terrain where the bush grows and how it is harvested (Darjeeling), and whether it ends up as bits in a bag (BOP, broken orange pekoe) or as a spoonful of well-formed whole leaf (TGFOP).

What isn't obvious is how these many-flavored teas *all* come from the very same generic plant, the *camellia sinensis* shrub: black, green, oolong, white, puehr (a compressed tea), and the rarely produced yellow tea. They begin from the same bush and end up so different without added ingredients, coloring, or chemicals – just leaf, air and heating.

This is worth emphasizing. Many people assume that there is a different plant for black, green and white teas. The colors are the result of how the leaf is handled. The teas start out the same. They end up diverse and contrasting: whole loose leaf versus dust in bags, strong black teas, light greens, smooth whites, aromatic oolongs, and earthy puehrs. There are more varieties of flavor than there are adjectives to capture them.

Every finished tea you buy is a variant on one of these five archetypal pictures. The obvious question is "So?" It's obvious that these teas look different and that they are likely to be just as dissimilar in taste and vary in price. Again: So?

| Whole leaf
Straight, twisted,
curled, balled | Cut, Tear, Curl
Machine processed
Pellets | Broken, fannings, dust
Tea sub-grades
Fragments | Puehr
Special handmaking
Brick, cake, bowl shapes | Herbal and flavored
Tea/substitute base
Additives |

The finished leaf that goes into your pot. None of the differences are cosmetic. They determine every element of taste and aroma.

The simplest but not too useful answer is "Try them and you'll see." Here are three more relevant comparisons that may help you decide if it's worth your trying them: cooking oils, hot dogs and wines.

The range of contrasts among teas that is discernable to the average palate corresponds closely to those of oils. There are strong qualitative gaps between vegetable oil, blended olive oil and extra virgin oil, and more subjective preferences within the main categories: sesame, peanut, canola and for olive oils a growing range of pedigrees: California first cold press, Tunisian, infused Chilean, raw unfiltered, etc. If you are at all choosy about your oils, it's worth being selective about your teas; you'll find the same types and degrees of difference and the same pleasure in finding ones that are a little special.

The hot dog comparison adds a dimension of certfication. Do you carefully read the ingredients to check on chemicals, "meat byproducts", country of origin, nitrites, fats, etc., with clear criteria for what you will consider buying and what you put back in the cooler? Then you should be careful in checking your tea, too: leaf quality, flavorings, filler material, freshness, pesticides, inspection, etc.

Many people who have a good sense of what's on the barbeque don't have a clue what they are drinking in their tea cup. That killer herbal brew may be quite literally just that. (No, that is not an exaggeration.)

The final comparison is with wine. Here the relevance is the payoff from knowing enough to explore the variety of affordable and accessible choices that enables you to find just what *you* like.

This doesn't mean becoming a connoisseur. "Enough" for you may mean to just have a sense of differences among, say, California, Washington State and Australian mid-price reds. You can confidently explore these to find great deals in the $25 range, or a lighter red that will go well with your Thanksgiving turkey. If you want to try the $250 ones with chateau names and vintages, it's your choice.

Teas are directly comparable to wines. If you mainly drink, say, a branded black tea in bags – the equivalent of house red – it will cost about a quarter a cup. If you pick out what it is you most like about it – strength, aroma, slight bitterness, its satisfying fullness, or lingering aftertaste, how many other black teas in the 20-50 cents a cup range are distinctly better in this characteristic? A conservative guesstimate is 200. How many do you know about? How well does your regular one compare?

Add in luxury teas at around $1 a cup; that makes another 100 or so choices. How many of these are available now from reliable online and tea specialty stores? All 300. How many are on the supermarket shelves? Perhaps 3 or 13, along with what can look like 333 boxes of near identical generic black tea bags.

The leaf: the tip of the bush at the top of the world

Below are pictures of the leaf. *At its best*. That needs emphasizing. Best implies there's a gradation from top to good, so-so, average and, of course, worst.

Best tea starts high, mostly on mountain slopes. Best leaf starts at the tip of the branch.

One word that captures "best" is that good tea is tiptop. The best leaf is at the tip of the branch at the top of the 2-4-foot-high bush and plucked with the tips of the fingers. The best leaf grows mostly on mountain slopes at the top of the world. It's harvested at the height of the season.

Tip and top are more than a play on words here. They are basic to understanding what makes, say, one English Breakfast special and another flat or bitter, why teas from Darjeeling in India, Yunnan in China and Japan's Uji region are so prized and very different from unprized ones farmed in Kenya or Argentina. Every single image in the collage above addresses some aspect of tea, where moving down means losing something, generally in the interests of lower costs.

The first top-left image shows the flourishing bush, with the shiny leaves whole and uniform: none of the blight and bite from the myriads of insects and bacteria that thrive in the wet, humid and warm seasons. Beneath it is the emblematic picture of "two leaves and a bud" that defines fine tea growing and harvesting. These are literally top quality.

The second column shows the variety of leaves, all from the same bush. The higher the degree of selectivity and specialization of planting and propagation, the more possibilities in the individualization of the tea. The third column is about tips: the hand plucking by skilled workers out on the slopes, where the seasonal mists, rain, winds and temperature shifts can create differences in flavors, sometimes within the same day.

And, finally, the economics of the tips: commonsense indicates that the Imperial plucking of just the most tender topmost bud and two leaves will yield much less harvest than moving down to a fine pluck and down even more to a coarse pluck.

These images capture the tradition of Artisan teas. Two leaves and a bud is both a description of the core of fine tea making and almost a natural law. No one has found a way to improve on it. Equally, though, it's becoming harder to make the profits needed to keep it alive.

Drop down a level and you are in the mass market of tea bags. The lower and flatter the farmland and the more of the bush that's picked, the lower the variety, richness of flavor, and special characteristics of the tea.

The two navigation paths: Artisan and Agribusiness

These differences among teas start from the harvesting and processing of the leaf. If it's selectively plucked by hand, that's in effect a commitment to nursing it to bring out its distinctive character, whereas grabbing and chopping it up blocks off the Artisan route.

Picking just the very top buds only in spring when they are most tender versus using lower leaves machine-gathered all year round obviously determines whether the tea is targeted to the supermarket bag or the specialty store tea chest.

In many instances, there is no real choice of path. The terrain, bush and leaf are not superior enough to command a premium position in the market and the competitive and financial strains make hand-crafted individualized quality tea unaffordable. To pick the obvious metaphor, this is a slippery slope. It's getting very crowded.

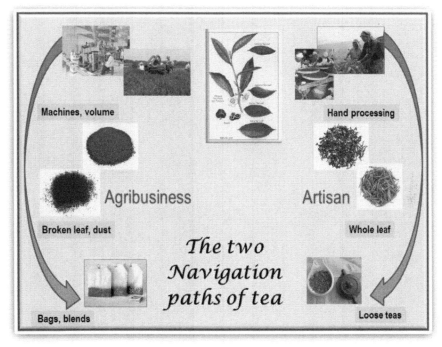

Agribusiness: branded packages of bags and tins of blends on the supermarket shelf
Artisan: more like fresh produce in a farmer's market, sold loose.

The key choice: Orthodox versus Cut, Tear, Curl

This is how to make fine Artisan tea. Note the dominance of people: doing the work, not just overseeing it. Even the final sorting is by hand. Machines are used in several stages, especially rolling the leaf, a process rather like drying clothes in a washing machine. They are often a century old.

The yellow behemoth in the center is a classical design, and surprisingly complex. Parts include a headend swivel bar, lotus plates, bent arms, rotating shaft and pneumatic cylinder. It meticulously modulates heat and moisture and delicately rotates heavy weights of leaf.

Artisan tea-making: hands and minds, not automation.

The images show the Artisan dilemma and contradiction: labor. Workers are inexpensive; this is the lowest wage large-scale industry in the world, with daily rates less than $2 and below official poverty levels. But at the same time they are too expensive: labor amounts to 60% of production costs; machines halve these. It's low level work, much of it contract workers hired seasonally. It's also very skilled: Two leaf and a bud plucking is not the same as lettuce picking. It demands experience, judgement, precision and dexterity. Workers are also becoming harder to find. With urbanization and the growth of manufacturing, the young are moving to the factories.

Here is how, in contrast to making Artisan whole leaf teas, to produce tea bags, blends, iced tea ingredients and cheap loose tea efficiently.

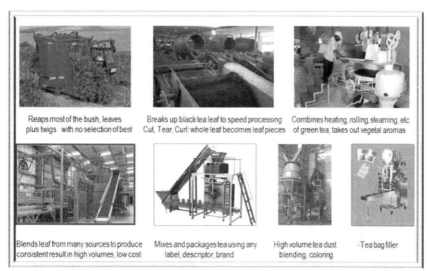

Reaps most of the bush, leaves plus twigs with no selection of best | Breaks up black tea leaf to speed processing Cut, Tear, Curl: whole leaf becomes leaf pieces | Combines heating, rolling, steaming, etc of green tea; takes out vegetal aromas

Blends leaf from many sources to produce consistent result in high volumes, low cost | Mixes and packages tea using any label, descriptor, brand | High volume tea dust blending, coloring | Tea bag filler

Agribusiness tea-making: automation, not hands and minds.

The operational differences between the two ways of making tea are visually obvious. Artisan production relies on people and fingers, while Agribusiness substitutes machines. The Artisan processes adapt to the leaf. Agribusiness manipulates the leaf to fit production.

For black teas, the basic choice that determines every later step is Orthodox processing versus Cut, Tear and Curl. Green teas are made differently, because they do not include the oxidation step that regulates the chemical interactions of the leaf with air. The tension is the same for all teas, as is the response: the labor-dependent Artisan-Orthodox method preserves the harvested leaf and moves it slowly through to the finished tea. Agribusiness-CTC speeds it by breaking it up, exploiting machines, standardization and streamlining.

This is analogous to butchers; "Orthodox" hand-cutting of steak permits more options in aging, grading and cooking than feeding it into a grinder to make ground beef. Once the chopping and mincing start, there's no going back. The analogy translates well visually. CTC looks like ground chuck in contrast to the strips of Orthodox leaf.

Shown below are teas that are clearly different from each other, except that they are the same: Assam blacks, from the largest tea growing region in the world. Assams are the base for strong black tea lends, especially English Breakfast.

The four single estate teas on the left side of the image are all whole leaf, the middle one CTC and the last one leaf dust. They are obviously varied in appearance but the differences go deeper than the visual and cosmetic, right down to the molecular structures that affect the exact richness, flavors and layers of tastes and aftertastes.

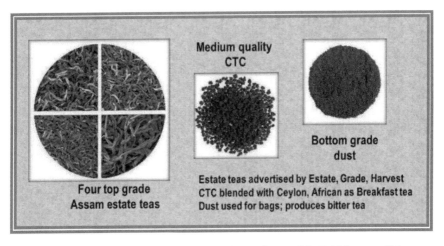

Teas from Assam, the largest producer region and core of the British tea tradition

An estate is a branded tea farm, the equivalent of a French wine chateau. The CTC in the center image is like "vin ordinaire": local, generic and a mix from many growers. There are minor variations in pellet size but it produces a reliable standard and basic ingredient for blending and packaging.

The teabag dust at the right is microscopic in size. It's like instant coffee: pour the water on the crystals and drink immediately, versus brew the ground beans. The highest compliment is "It tastes like real coffee." Alas, the Agribusiness slippery slope has lowered the tea standard of comparison, so that we don't say that a tea bag tastes like "real tea." It's become the dominant seller and hence is the "real" thing for many casual tea drinkers. Tea equals bag and bag equals tea.

Amazon provides a summary of how many teas are marketed as "Assam." It lists 23 thousand tea bags and just over a thousand loose leaf ones. The obvious question as you sip your morning tea is: So what? Whole leaf, CTC, dust... Why should I even have to know which I'm buying? If they are all Assam, I'll choose by the price, convenience, brand and anything else that grabs me – I like the envelopes the XYZ bags come in and I always enjoy my ZYX tins of tea.

This raises some counterquestions:

Do you know what the differences are that affect your own enjoyment? You may find the bagged breakfast tea bag you drink more harsh than you'd like and put up with it as common among Assams, without realizing that this is far more a basic element of tea dust.

The larger surface area of the dust releases the compounds that give tea its fullness of flavor very quickly. The whole leaf balances the flow with the other molecules that add aroma, mellowness, and subtle overtones. Teabag dust makes for a rough or bland brew. Would you ever order an instant coffee cappuccino? Do you even like instant?

Do you even know which "Assam" you are drinking? It probably has never occurred to you to look. You may then assume that a tin of CTC is a better deal than it really is and be unaware that there are a lot of far more interesting Assams to try out.

If this is the style of black tea you like, are you missing out on special deals? Tea marketing too often persuades buyers to pick a package just because it's an "Assam" but they don't realize that this indicates a style not a quality. They need to know about the leaf and often don't because they stick to tea bags.

Amazon shows two teas from the very same vendor, literally next to each other on the Web page: a "CTC Exotic (Blend)" for $3.50 an ounce (30 cents a cup) and a clonal second flush from a superb estate, Halmari.

At $3.50 an ounce, 30 cents a cup, the CTC is a so-so buy.

The Halmari is a stunning one for *less*: $2.80, 25¢ a cup.

This simple example points to the question that *Tea Tips* aims to answer for you: What is it helpful to know about when you're shopping for tea? The starting point always is to focus on the leaf. Which comes back to the Artisan and Agribusiness paths and the so different results that each creates. Why is the Halmari such a stellar tea and the CTC Exotic just an OK one? What happens en route from bush to cup?

The rotorvane: Crush! Rip! Macerate!

The key no-going-back step in CTC comes between the withering of the harvested leaf to reduce its moisture and the oxidation to build its flavors and the color of the tea. Orthodox processing lightly rolls the leaf to start breaking up its cells and releasing enzymes to catalyze oxidation. CTC launches a full force assault.

The rotorvane: aircraft engine size and pretty much the same engineering

The central machine is the rotorvane, a set of fast and powerful rotary drum cylinders spinning in opposite directions. The teeth "macerate" the leaf after first conditioning it to clean it up so it can be fed in a continuous stream; secondary leaf and the broken pieces and dust are recycled into the flow. The rotorvanes shape the leaf into pellets of uniform size; rollers with sharp grooved cutters reshape it to look leaf-ish. The crushers and tearers operate at speeds of up to 5,000 revolutions per minute. The larger machines can macerate

2,500 kilograms of leaf, 5,500 pounds.

This is a very efficient process and without its expansion in the 1950s the black tea industry could not have remained economically viable for the mass market. It cuts processing time in half, produces a fuller, darker and largely more bitter brew, and gets a higher yield per hectare of bushes.

It is far more cost-effective, especially when combined with machine-harvesting. CTC is used to make 85% of all black tea which comprises around 80% of the global market. Something must get lost in all this: complexity of flavor. The core driver of every move from Artisan to Agribusiness is standardization. That means reducing variance and establishing a baseline average.

The owner of one of the best estates in Darjeeling, Goomtee, captures what determines the teas that get into the mass outlets and those that don't and won't: "The [largest global brands] are blenders and packagers – so they can never provide good recognition to individual gardens and boutique properties. The major blenders buy medium quality teas to make a standard tea so that they can offer a consistent blend at all locations twelve months in a year."

This statement succinctly summarizes the main theme of *Tea Tips*: if you like what's standard on the grocery store shelf, you can still do much better. Goomtee alone makes more varieties of Darjeeling as just one of almost a hundred gardens than you will find in any grocery or supermarket anywhere.

Tea Tips could accurately add a subtitle of *Beyond the Teabag*. It's not that supermarket teas aspire to mediocrity and rarely reach it, or that many are misleadingly advertised and overpriced, or that their "natural" flavors mean only that these can be found somewhere in natural form: wood pulp, for instance, and extract of... no, you really don't want to know just what some of the legal ones are.

The broader issue is that they represent such a narrow subset of teas. They are never better in flavor in dust, pellet and broken leaf form than whole leaf. If you like the teas you know about and regularly drink, with just a little information to guide you can find much better choices. The Assam example is illustrative.

An example of the Artisan craft at its best: Dragonwell

Location plus pedigree plus culture

Here's an illustration of how the best pedigree teas are made. While not typical in all its ultra-ultraprecision, it shows the motivation and methods of the craft. The tea is Dragonwell, traditionally served in a glass to highlight the unfolding of the leaf as it brews.

Dragonwell, Longjing: Consensually rated the best of all China teas.

Dragonwell is one of the most noted of all green teas across the globe. It comes from Longjing, a small village area in China with ideal tea terrain. This is less remote than many of the comparable – and truly spectacular – prestigious tea areas across the world, but it shares their common feature: mountain slopes that provide the seasonality, moisture, soil conditions and temperature variations to produce the very best leaf.

What makes Dragonwell unique is its combination of terrain and craft tradition, plus the commitment to preserving both. The terroir is like the great wine regions of, say, Bordeaux, Rioja and Barolo. Each signals a distinctive style and characteristic of wine. Around them, a work, business and community culture grows that evolves methods, networks and skills.

Dragonwell is comparable in this regard to, say, the Vosne-Romanée commune in Burgundy that produces red wines, mostly from the pinot noir grape. Other regions of China now grow Dragonwell varieties, just as there are plenty of California Burgundies, and many small farmers produce variants in the areas surrounding Longjing. These range widely in quality with some excellent buys and, alas, many "inauthentic" imitations, fakes and adulterations. (Disney Epcot used to sell in its China pavilion gift shop a very strange Lung Ching Dragonwell package of 100 tea bags (!) for less than $9 (!!). Mickey Mouse tea seems a fair description.

Super-super Longjing Dragonwell grades sell at luxury prices, just like rare vintages of wine and often for the same reasons: social display and very conspicuous consumption. One of the residual traditions in China is the ritual of gift-giving in business, politics and formal society. Prestigious tea of noted and even notorious expense draws the appropriate nods of approval for giver and getter.

But you can expect to pay just 40 cents a cup for a very satisfying Dragonwell. That's worth emphasizing. One of the most famous and sought after teas in the world costs a few cents more than a tea bag that has far less of every element of tea quality and flavor.

The calendar is a critical component of Dragonwell production and quality. The rarest imperial grade leaf is plucked up on Lion's Peak only on the first of the ten days of the pre-Qingming festival, just before the seasonal spring rains begin.

Three common elements of the great teas: Slopes, with careful soil and water management, absolutely fresh and unblemished leaf, and biodiversity.

Those farms are tiny: the Chinese government allocates a sixth of an acre per family member living under the same roof on Lion's Peak. That means that many are just a single acre: three quarters of a football field. That will produce maybe sixty pounds of finished tea. The best growers can command a corresponding price premium.

Ancient and modern: a thousand years of continuity

There are references to Dragonwell tea as early as the eighth century, and it was formally given its name in the thirteenth. Around 1750, the Qing Dynasty emperor set aside 18 bushes, with the leaf plucked during just a single day a year. He gave it Imperial Gong Fu status as a Tribute tea. You can guess who got the tribute.

The 18 Imperial tea bushes   *The Emperor*   *For the tourists, but authentic*

In Imperial times, young virgins, wearing gold gloves and using gold scissors, delicately plucked the stem and placed it into a gold basket. The dragon well was famed for the purity of its water according to varying legends, including the one that starts out with some monk visiting a local dragon to get it to help break a drought. So, the dragon... Yeah, whatever.

China tea lore is a mix of genuine historical trends, fleshed out as fables and then romanticized for purposes of modern marketing. They add to the mystique – and to the price. Ignore them. The virgins and gold accoutrements are long past; the growers ran out of one or the other, or both.

But the steps remain very much the same. The original bushes still thrive in a tourist Imperial Tea Garden. So far, bans on pesticides have kept the mountain rainwater pristine. Climate change is an ever-looming threat, of course. The industrial smog from Hangzhou is a related concern. Pesticide use is creeping in.

What still has relevance from mythic history is how this long heritage has been maintained and sustained for 1,200 years, at the very least. This hints at the core of the Artisan tradition: pragmatic refinement of what has worked and that continues to do so, adapting to the seasons and renewing the richness of the terrain and the bushes. It's very conservative, bounded by locale and culture, small in scale, and built on adaptive skills derived from experience. Almost by definition, it can never be mass production.

There are around seventy growers, merchants, and trading companies nested around Longjing. Local regulation and cooperation are strong, including "unified packaging rules" to protect against counterfeiting. (The solution indicates the problem, which is endemic with all the great names in tea.)

Like many of the pedigree tea growing highland regions, Longjing is a popular tourist attraction, combining history, scenery, ethnic costumes, wildlife preserves, Buddhist temples, and artefacts. It's unique among China's most prestigious tea-growing regions by being close to one of its largest cities, Hangzhou. Should you plan to visit China, it is well worth putting it high on your itinerary. This is a UNESCO Heritage site and has long been a center of history, the arts and garden design – and tea growing.

Crafting the tea

Dragonwell remains very good indeed. The historical strengths have been preserved and the scenery conserved: no monster machines harvesting the slopes or condos on the hilltops. Producing it is selective, labor-intensive and slow. In a ten-hour day, a Longjing tea plucker gathers 4-5 pounds of leaf, 80,000 individual buds of uniform 1-2 centimeter size. That makes just one pound of finished Dragonwell.

It is a light green tea, with a fresh and crisp vegetal flavor and long-lingering aftertaste. There's not a hint of bitterness. The top grades are more uniform and consistent in color and shape. They are smoother and the flavors and aroma more pronounced.

Just how much "more" is discernable to you is a matter of your palate and taste preferences. The medium grades of Longjing Dragonwell are really satisfying and the lower ones fine, though less long-lasting in taste and with a shorter freshness in storage.

Plucking the bushes sets the cost and quality parameters. It is a surprisingly complex activity that involves much more than just snapping off the top of the bush. Chinese growers distinguish multiple levels of plucking. The Imperial pluck gathers just the top bud and leaf, while a fine pluck picks the two leaves.

The issue is not simply how to harvest the leaves – the very nature of the highland slopes make machines impractical – but how to pick the very best buds at the very best time and in the very best weather conditions. The plucker must avoid bruising the leaf, squeeze instead of snapping the stem, and reject any purple or frayed tips. This is not done at a leisurely pace. The hands move very quickly and precisely. A single day's work adds up to thirty thousand wrist actions.

Try picking a needle from a haystack. Pluck it, don't smush it.

The better the terrain, then the better the leaf on the bush in terms of nutrients, the myriad of compounds that give it flavor and make it healthy, and the potential for drawing out special characteristics. The better the plucking, the greater the opportunity for the tea maker to shape, refine and balance the many elements that produce a Dragonwell or any of the other great teas.

When you buy tea, this is the fundamental equation: quality is a function of what's on the bush and how this is selected and harvested. Machines have been used for a century for completely routine steps that involve no judgement, variances and quality challenges. But these do not change the basics of the leaf. The moment the leaf is machine-plucked or chopped up by the sharp jaws of a rotorvane, the tea is entirely different.

Hence, the overall processes of Artisan teas like Dragonwell remain old-fashioned, inefficient and labor-intensive. But today and for the near future, a machine-made Longjing Dragonwell would mean changing paths, from Artisan variety to Agribusiness standardization.

There is simply no way that the machine-harvesting of green tea shown below (in Borneo) and the China automated processing factory can create a Dragonwell, Mao Feng, Moonlight white or Darjeeling estate black that has the range of flavors, textures, nuances and individual subtleties as the estimated forty distinct Dragonwells.

The two leaves and a bud never get a fighting chance.

Here's one global giant's description of its operations: "The company *reprocesses instant teas...* in its *Florida* factory, by *changing physical parameters* such as density, particle size, making *formulations with flavors and sweeteners*, or blending them with *other food ingredients.*" But it markets its teas as the opposite of the highlighted words. One message for Wall Street and one for shoppers.

It sells green tea bags with pedigree names that make them sound directly comparable with Longjing Dragonwell, but this is a different business. "Changing physical parameters" applies to both Artisan and Agribusiness teas, but with different meanings and methods relating to changing, physical and parameters. Artisan methods are not a quaint historical artefact. They remain the best way to make the best teas, though not to make mass market branded beverages.

That best way continues immediately after the plucking. The Dragonwell leaf is spread out and withered for 8-10 hours, with careful attention to heat and humidity. It is then pan-fired (or fried: the terms are interchangeable) in two stages lasting 30-100 minutes, with the temperature adjusted in removing the moisture in the leaf.

The delicate and light firing is done with bare hands so that the worker senses the temperature of the wok and leaf texture in adjusting the process. It takes three years to learn the ten distinct hand movements involved. Only four ounces of leaf are fired at a time. Lower grades are fried in a hotter wok, longer and with heavier hand pressure.

All Artisan teas are variants on this hands-on sequence. It begins in the field.

Choosing and buying Dragonwell

Dragonwell tea is easy to locate online and in specialty shops. Prices are competitive and there is plenty of variety. Quality is more iffy to judge. Even for experts, it can be a challenge. Many sellers have coopted terms and added letters and labels to the official and complex self-regulated formal grading system – Grade A, Imperial, Grade 3, Pre-Qingming, Bird's Tongue, Competition Grade, Superior, Lotus Heart, etc.

Much of what you'll come across in local specialty stores is not fresh but bulk wholesaler tea with limited quality assurance and pedigree. It's still more flavorful and less bitter than Agribusiness green monsters, but with Dragonwell the nuances of flavors cover such a range that it's worth spending extra for one of the higher grades.

The commonsense quality tests for the non-professional are does the tea look fresh – Dragonwell is distinctly bright in appearance – and is it of consistent form and size and not full of broken pieces and twigs? These are helpful mostly in eliminating poor quality teas but at the higher end, it's essential to find a trusted supplier.

In general, the best sources are the online specialists with a strong presence in the region of origin, relationships with growers and export-licensed agents, and precise descriptions of the tea, without poetry and hype. Reliable sellers provide an accurate representation of what they offer and their inventory is generally the better grades, though not the rarest and luxury specials.

There's a definite problem in the tea industry of fakes. Dragonwell is as vulnerable to this as any of the prestigious teas that command a premium price for a premium reputation. One trick is to mix a lower grade leaf into a top one. Shining up a drab leaf with chemicals or relabeling a "Dragonwell" from another growing region as Longjing is not uncommon, alas.

You can get a good idea of the likely quality of the teas a provider sells by what the site's Home and About Us pages highlight. Customer reviews are helpful not so much in the number of stars they give but the knowledge that they themselves show in their evaluations. They can offer useful pointers to quality and special characteristics.

One general *Tea Tips* rule is look not just for what is stated but at what is omitted. Dragonwell should be clearly and reliably identified as grown in Longjing, Hangzhou in Zhejiang Province. Omitted, assume it's from one of the other China provinces that offer their own, sometimes good but mostly so-so. Or Taiwan or Vietnam. If the leaf and grade are not apparent, there's a reason.

One example is from Amazon's list of over 300 Dragonwell choices. It's a whole pound of tea for under $30, which is just about the price per cup, 15 cents, for a ho-hum tea bag. It's simply nonsensical to accept that a top hand-crafted tea could sell for this price. It must be dross.

But, of course, it gets the marketing gloss over. The ad starts off with Dragonwell is great, historical and named for the well in Longjing. Then comes accurate information about two leaves and a bud and, as ever, the long tradition of the very, very, best Dragonwell being harvested by certified virgins for just three days in the year. "Plucking has changed since then." Ah. That is a way of saying without saying that this stuff is not crafted the old way.

The sales pitch finishes off with the evocative mixed metaphors and lyricism of "the bud and shoots presenting themselves, looking like they are about to be plucked by the young virgins." And what look is that? The ingredients are "green tea from China." At a guess, this is either a Yunnan province tea or from the border of Zhejiang Province and neighboring Fujian. If it's Yunnan, it may be decent. If it's Zhejiang, it could be more than a teensy bit enhanced with pesticides. There is no way to tell here.

But do read the ingredients. The information they include is legally bounded but the marketing, name, branding, images and embellishments are open to poetic imagination and what Winston Churchill called a terminological inexactitude, not exactly un-truthful but not quite fact-packed. The ingredient list must omit. not fudge. When it states "green tea from China" that is directly equivalent to "this is not from Longjing and it's not worth naming."

Look for a seller that describes the tea in plain terms: exactly where it's from, how it is grown and harvested, and what are its distinctive characteristics of taste and aroma. Is this at the level where it makes sense to you and doesn't demand an act of faith in accepting and believing it? The moment you see images and ad-speak substituting for facts, it is best to move on.

Whether you enjoy Dragonwell or not, there are plenty of other excellent comparable Artisan teas to pick from, made in the same way and to the same standards. This example happens to be a green tea from China. But with variations of detail, all the descriptions of terrain, harvesting and processing could be of other green teas, including Japanese sencha, oolongs from Taiwan, Darjeelings from India, estate teas from Sri Lanka, and the elite white teas from China.

They all are representative of the best and while they can be very expensive indeed for the equivalents of Chateau d'Yquem, they are very affordable. And just how much is that latte?

Tea myths and misconceptions

Here are ten widespread myths about tea. If you take them as truths, you'll end up disliking or just putting up with tea, overpaying, being ripped off, or missing out on attractive choices.

THE MYTH	THE REALITY
1 Tea is bitter	*Only if you brew it too long*, at the wrong temperature. The most common complaint about tea and the easiest to fix.
2 Specialty tea is pricy	*You don't have to pay a luxury price*. Most Artisan teas cost 25-40 cents a cup. A medium quality tea bag is 15-25¢. The most outstanding teas almost all go for less than 75¢.
3 Tea bags are just as good as whole leaf	*They are rarely a "leaf"* but broken pieces, "fannings" and "dust," with most of the aromas and flavor lost. They are hot dog meat, not filet.
4 Green tea cures illness, cuts weight	*Not proven*. Research suggests that tea offers many health benefits but there is no scientific proof. Buy good tea for its taste; if there are such benefits you'll get them anyway.
5 English tea is superior	*There is no such thing*. English names are packagers, not producers, of mainly Indian, African and Sri Lankan blends. Don't fall for fake aristocratic heritage. It adds $$, not quality. Focus on where the tea comes from.
6 "Natural" and "organic" teas are special	*"Natural" means found somewhere in nature* and includes even sawdust. "Organic" excludes lead contamination. Ignore the label: look at reputation and pedigree. All Artisan tea is naturally natural.
7 Green teas have the least caffeine	*On average, yes*. But there are more variations within a type of tea – black, green, white – than across them. Tea has around 1/3 the caffeine of coffee. It doesn't make much difference what color of tea you choose.
8 Most tea is from India and China	*Most low-end tea is from Argentina (green) and Kenya (black).* Most of the best is made in Taiwan, Japan, Nepal, and Sri Lanka, plus China and India. Choose by locale and how the leaf is harvested and processed.
9 You can store tea anywhere	*Store it in tins with tight lids*. Never in the fridge or by the stove. Tea is highly absorbent, interacts eagerly with air, heat, light and odors.
10 Tea is best with milk and sugar	*The better the tea, the less it needs them*. Milk was mostly used to soften and cool harsh black tea. Sugar is part of many tea cultures and very much a personal choice.

Myth 1. Tea is bitter

Only if you torture it to death by brewing it too long at too high a temperature, or in a microwave oven. Or buy cheap machine-mowed lowland tea that includes broken pieces, twigs and leaves from much further down the bush from the nutritious buds.

Bitterness is both the most widespread complaint about tea and the easy problem to fix. You are generally the cause.

So, be the cure; it's simple. *Look after the water and the tea will look after itself.* Here are four rules:

Use water that is neutral in terms of acid and alkaline levels. Most tap water is slightly acidic and soft. Avoid hard water with any taste of minerals. Filtered is preferable. Bottled is unreliable.

Heat the water to the temperature best suited to the leaf: high for blacks, lower for greens. The range is from 170-212 degrees. Greens brewed at boiling point will be nastily bitter and blacks tepidly heated at the lower end flat and lacking flavor.

Do not touch the microwave. Treat the oven as a tomb where teas go only to die. The physics of "boiling" water in microwaves are akin to bomb-making.

Just follow some simple brewing times and temperatures, shown in this summary table for different types of tea. Most people don't have access to a portable thermometer, so it includes guidelines on how long to leave the water after it has boiled to cool to the required temperature. The best tea makers have a built-in time/temp setting.

Type	Temp (°F)	Time (mins)	No thermometer
Black	205-212	3-5	Boil, wait a few seconds
Green	170-185	1.5-3	Boil, cool 3 minutes
Oolong	195	3-4	Boil, cool 2 minutes
White	175	3-4	Boil, cool 3 minutes

That's it. If you buy a decent quality tea and follow these rules, it won't be bitter. Temperature and time affect every single dynamic of the subtle and complex chemistry of tea that involves at least six hundred molecular compounds. The tea maker produces a brew for your pot and cup that balances their interactions – if you stick to the rules.

Astringency is not bitterness

Tea is naturally astringent. This is the dry taste that is also a characteristic of wines, leafy greens and crunchy apples. It adds that little zip to the drink and stimulates the senses. The words that capture it have the association of pleasantly energizing: brisk, tangy, zesty, tippy and wake-up. It's generated by the tannins in the leaf.

"Tannin" is a word with negative connotations because it is widely assumed to refer to tannic acid, found in leather and made from oak leaves used to prepare the materials, creating a subliminal identification with tanning. But there's none of this in tea. The tannins are natural and healthy organic chemicals in the leaf.

They are found in many vegetables and fruits, and most herbs and spices contain them. Tannins also form in slow-moving rivers through the decay of vegetal matter; the one in the image below is noted for its pristine beauty and is red with tannins. (Opanara in New Zealand.)

Two very different tannins: the natural in vegetables that colors river water harmlessly: dyes extracted from bark and acorns to treat leather

Released slowly and gently, natural tannins add to the richness of a tea's flavor and aftertaste while all the other compounds are creating their own special interactions. Released quickly and at a higher temperature, they give the tea its body and strength. This is directly comparable to wines where the lightness of a Beaujolais, acidity of a dry white and fullness of a red Rioja come from the inclusion or removal of skins, stems and seeds after harvesting. Their fermentation lets the tannins bind to proteins and build "mouthfeel."

Making a good pot of tea means balancing time and the dynamic complexity of the chemistry of the leaf. When you brew green tea at too high a temperature for too long, such as in the microwave, the tannins overwhelm the entire drink. By reducing the temperature, you allow the "umami" – sweetness – compounds to build. If you leave a black tea bag stewing, all you are letting it do is transfer more tannins. It has less sweetness and much more astringency. You commit negligent tea-icide.

Water temperature aids the synchronization of the interactions of polyphenols and tannins. Polyphenols are a store of time-release compounds that dissolve at different rates. The processing of the leaf creates varied amounts of the key ones, which break down into myriads of tongue twisters like quercetin, ishoramnetin and kaempferol.

The most important in brewing are catechins plus theaflavins and thearubigins. Very roughly, catechins contribute to the lightness and sweetness of the tea and the others to its fullness. Black and green teas have a very different balance of these. Brewing must nurse the catechins and tame the body builders. What's *in* the leaf is a given; what comes *out* is a managed process. Think of it this way. Do you steam your steak? If cooking it were just a matter of heat, that's as good a technique as any. It's not. Nor is tea making just a matter of boiling water.

The details of all this are exquisitely complex at the molecular level but the brewing temp/times guidelines are a pragmatic and reliable simplification for regulating the rate and extent of the compounds dissolving in the pot. Adjust the specifics to meet your personal preferences but only within very narrow ranges. The general rule for black teas, for example, is boiling water at 212°F. 205° is fine in most instances, but at 200° you'll sense a slight loss of zip.

Don't play around with green teas; they are carefully cultivated and nurtured to release their flavor at 170-185° and artfully tailored to punish the taste buds of those who trespass outside the heat limits. Japanese greens are the most finicky here; a good fukamushi (deep-steamed) sencha should be made at 150°/1.5 minutes versus 160°/1.5 for a light-steamed asamushi. At 170°/2.5 minutes both these teas are transformed from exquisite to truly execrable.

In general, a useful subrule is that when you are not satisfied with a tea, don't increase the steeping time. If it is too weak, add more leaf in your next brewing. For harsh, overstrong teas, cut back on amount, time and/or hotness. With tea, less is generally better. It's ironic that in our age where, in Carrie Fisher's piquant epigram, the trouble with instant gratification is that it's just not fast enough, so many tea drinkers delay getting their gratification by brewing it for as long as ten minutes. When in doubt, choose three minutes.

Tea bags throw off all calculations. The ingredients are generally chosen to handle a wide range of water temperatures and to provide a strong burst of flavor that can quickly get through the porous barrier of the bag itself. Their fannings and dust present a large surface area for the tannin to infuse the water, whereas whole leaf tea unfolds more slowly. Leave the bag in the tea for extra minutes and the tannins voraciously seek out more tastemates.

A quick scan of online recommendations for teabags shows no consensus: 4-8 minutes is typical and 6-8 occasional, along with 1-2. Again, for those who do drink tea bags, the suggestion is less not more: shorter times.

Choosing the water

Always find good water. "Good" here means as close to being pure as makes sense. For tea experts, the available water is never good enough. They want the equivalent of a pristine mountain stream. There is no need to go to such an extreme for the teas you are likely to drink daily, even if it were practical. But rare ones, especially the subtlest whites and greens, demand meticulous preparation and a very discriminating palate. They deserve water that brings out the best of the taste and taster.

The more general aim is simply to ensure that you experience the flavors and aromas that the tea producer intended. The priority is to avoid hard water that is high in minerals; that's generally easy to spot from the taste or by its leaving a light film across the surface. Soft water makes for flat-tasting tea, so avoid distilled water with its low minerals. You need a neutral pH acidity level of around 7.

Water from the faucet is fully adequate in many regions, though it is sometimes affected by minerals, old pipes, chlorine and occasional nasties. The practical home choice is simply to add a filter to your faucet. Using bottled water is generally less satisfactory. It's expensive and the market is unregulated and notoriously prone to shady practices. That said, the large bottles of spring water that are part of the office coffee and teabag scenery are reliable.

One expert offers a simple general rule. He found no consistent differences in ratings for the same tea brewed with tap, filtered, gourmet bottled and bottled spring water. He comments that if you wouldn't use your tap water as a regular drink, then don't make tea with it.

This sounds simple and is. But most tea drinkers aren't aware of just how critical water is in making tea. They too often casually put the cup in a microwave to heat the water without realizing that this can only achieve the worst results, with zero chance of other than an awful brew.

Microwaving tea water: the worst option by far

The wide literature, both popular and scientific, on making tea in a microwave is very entertaining. The consensual opinion is it's generally OK, but not really. You have no control over the temperature, and you can't tell if the water is going to hiss, bang or explode when you add a bag. There is a wee whiff of toxic gas created when you nuke polystyrene, though "It won't kill you, but I wouldn't do it on a regular basis", "Plastic [cups] don't play nice in the microwave", and, a personal favorite: "What's that white foam I get on my tea?" (*Tea Tips* will spare you the trick for brewing tea that melts the strofoam; it's fun, though.)

Microwaving doesn't "boil" water. It's rather like Stars Wars Stormtroopers randomly zapping four-second jolts that create "nucleation points." A kettle uniformly builds heat from the bottom up in an even and smooth flow through the water. Microwaving leaves some areas cold and others invisibly higher than the 212° boiling point. Or not. As you can guess, if the Stormtroopers hit that little metal staple on the tea bag...

All this creates some very complicated reactions that include superheating (turns your cup into a steam grenade), loss of oxygen (blands the tea down to insipid) and accentuation of the taste of impurities from the water and even the cup material.

There's some striking evidence, too, that microwaving water leaches out its nutrients. It's shown by a simple experiment that has been repeated many times. Two identical seedling plants in identical soil are treated over 7-9 days, one with water that has been microwaved and the other with purified water that was boiled in a kettle. From Day 1 on, the results are consistent. Microwaved water starves the plant. Here's Day 7:

Two plants fed with microwaved and faucet water.
Day 7: one dead and one thriving.

This strongly suggests that the water isn't exactly a stimulant to your tea leaf's building and releasing its flavors.

If you enjoy tea as more than a hydrator and morning energizer, it really is worth following the four rules. Obviously, that's trickier on the road or in the office versus at home. The ideal is a filter on your faucet, a cheap kettle, a pot or infuser to brew tea in, your wrist watch for timing, and a good ceramic or glass cup. You don't have these in your pocket or bag.

But you can carry the tea with you – and it doesn't have to be in a bag. All you need is a small basket infuser and a small tight container. In the office, you have access to the standard large flagon of spring water in the coffee room and a way of heating the water. That may require you to store a small plastic kettle/heater in the office.

It's worth it. The corollary of look after the water and the tea will look after itself is that if you don't look after the water, the tea can't deliver the taste and flavor. Here are three simple options for the traveling tea kit that, while they don't help you find the water, make it much easier for you to brew tea accurately and conveniently wherever you may be.

Portable accessories for teabag convenience but whole leaf tea: basket, tumbler, equivalent of toiletries bag

The infuser basket fits in the cup and is a very inexpensive convenience, as much so as a teabag. The double-walled safety glass tumbler in the middle image has its own removable infuser. It's pretty much an essential for commuting. The travel kit on the right is more of a special indulgence. It's a small Japanese style kettle and "gong fu" set, ideal for brewing the oolongs and whites that fit into the spacious enough case. Just add water.

Myth 2. Specialty tea is pricy

Good whole leaf tea is much less expensive that most people assume and tea bags conversely are often packaged to look cheaper than they are. There is only one useful measure for comparing tea prices: cost per cup. The multiple standard weights and measures are not immediately translatable to "How much is this versus this or that?" when the first "this" is 125 grams and the second a box of 18 tea bags, sitting next to a "or that?" containing 4 ounces.

Tea bags come in packages of 15, 18, 20, 24 and all the way up to 312. The only and intriguing pattern is that they never come in prime number units. Tins of tea are typically 100 grams (3.5 oz), 4 ounces and 125 grams (4.1) and loose leaf tea sells in ounces, 30 gram samples (1.06 oz), and kilos (2.2 lbs.) This mishmash makes it bewildering in determining what a tea actually costs.

Even a "cup" is ambiguous. Most traditional tea set ones hold around five ounces, Asian cups four, and gongfu cups between one and two. Breakfast cups in western teaware are larger. Tea mugs are 10 ounces, but 12-ounce coffee/tea ones are common. An 8-ounce cup may really be 6 ounces since it is rarely filled to the very top.

The consensual measure used across the industry is how much a tea costs per standard 6-ounce coffee cup, assuming 1 tea bag makes a cup and that, for leaf tea measured out in spoonfuls, you get 200 cups per pound, 12.5 per ounce. Here's the resulting simple base for comparing bags, ounces and grams.

1 bag	1 ounce	1 pound	100 grams	125 grams	1 kilo
1 cup	12 cups	200 cups	40 cups	50 cups	450 cups

Key comparative figure: 1 teabag = 1 cup, 1 whole leaf ounce = 12 cups
Typical online deal is for 40 cups, 100 grams (3.5 ounces)

It's very much a baseline measure and not exact. Some loose teas are bulkier or heavier than the norm. Most need just one spoonful of loose leaf per cup but others closer to two, whites especially. Larger leaf teas that are not fully oxidated can be infused several times while tea bags while most Artisan black teas are used to make a single cup, with maybe a topup. Then there are your own personal preferences for how strong you want the tea to be.

The relative differences even out. Though the white is lighter than the black, when you take a spoonful it will naturally be more heaped and puffy than a level one of the Ceylon. The cents per cup metric provides a good mental check on comparative costs. Here are useful rules of thumb:

Tea bags of medium to good quality tea cost 15-25 cents each. Bags are sold by the box, mostly in units of 15-24.
Agribusiness blends sold in supermarkets generally cost 20-30 cents a cup. They are largely sold in 3-4 ounce tins.
Artisan teas are mostly in the 20-50 cent range. They are priced by the ounce or measures of grams. The 50-80 cent bracket includes many of the best known and most outstanding names. Above that are luxury rarities where, like grand cru wines, prices can be headline-provoking.

The three tables below convert purchase units into cost per cup.

LOOSE PER OZ LB		LOOSE TINS 100 X 125 GRAMS			TEA BAGS BAGS PER PACKAGE		
PRICE	¢ CUP	PRICE	100 GM	125 GM	PRICE	15	20	24
$2 ($32)	16¢	$6	14¢	11¢	$3	20¢	15¢	13¢
3 (48)	24	8	18	14	4	27	20	17
4 (64)	32	10	22	18	5	33	25	21
5 (80)	40	15	34	24	8	53	40	33
8 (128)	64	20	44	36	10	66	50	42

$4 for 1 oz of loose tea is average for good grades: 32 cents a cup
Equivalent cost is $15 for 100 gm, $20 for 125 gm. $5 for 15 bags, $8 for 24

The figures can be a little muddling, which reflects the intentional muddle of most tea marketing – make the average stuff look cheaper than it is and the premium brands look better quality than they are.

The tables illustrate the key difference between price and price point. There's a big mental gap between the two. The price point is the purchase amount: $3.29 for the package of bags, $79.75 for a pound of Darjeeling, or $16.99 for a tin of flavored floral blends.

The Agribusiness tea industry is very candid in its selling strategies. It's packaging first, foremost, central, critical, creative and dominant. Most tea buyers therefore check out the box or tin first – does this look good? – and then respond not so much to the unit price as the price point – is this in the right range? The figure is easy for the customer to assess, meets expectations and sets a threshold. It accounts for the plethora of "Only $9.99" deals – not $9.92 or $10.15.

So, for example, tea bags in the $3-4 a box price point count as "cheap" and $15 as "gourmet" without much further evaluation. That's how you end up paying far more than you should for mediocre tea. Lots more. One of the good but not great high end consumer brands offers a "presentation" box of twenty blah teas in pyramid bags for $28.50. That's a total of two ounces of tea that you can get for $5 anywhere. The packaging probably costs $2.

The entire carton and the wrappings are stunning and radiate cool elegance. The logic here is that the presentation creates the value, not the tea. The tea is made gourmet by a few dollars of cardboard and color – it must be great because it's so elegant. This strategy rests on customer ignorance. What was that about the Emperor's new clothes?

This package/price point sales pitch is most marked with tins, where a wholesaler blends an anonymous mix of leaf from many sources, some quite good but rarely Artisan quality, in a beautifully designed container, tailored to the seller's specifications. You could travel round US museums, theme parks and public institutions, collecting their "specially made for us" Colonial Bohea, Imperial Blend" in the same attractive black tin with its name on the antique-looking label. Line them up; all that's different is their name: yours.

Whole leaf tea sells on its merits rather than its packaging. Yes, some of the snob appeal stores use ambience to suggest the tea is as unique as the setting. Just check their price per cup versus those in a quick sample of good online sellers. Yes, some top end tea prices are off the scale and in the personal luxury class. You need a loaded wallet and an excellent palate to appreciate the recently advertised $40 an ounce for a Castleton estate Darjeeling ($640 a pound, $3 a cup). A London restaurant has gained press coverage for its Da Hong Pao ("Big Red Robe") served for $300 a cup. That's absurd, of course, but the very fact that it is straight-faced plausible illustrates the ways that tea is marketed through mystique and reverence.

This all add cachet to the impressions of tea as upper class and for the sophisticated elite. It gives a misleading view of your own choices: that you must spend a large amount of money to get good teas, and by inference that lower priced ones are slightly second-rate. There is no doubt that just a few cups of, say, the superb Adam's Peak white tea from Sri Lanka is a memory to treasure. That runs for about $350 a pound ($1.80 a cup.) But it's representative of nothing but itself, perhaps like a $2,700 Louis XIII cognac.

Just for reference: *Tea Tips'* author pays on average 30 cents a cup for most of his fairly extensive stock of sixty or so teas. There are plenty of bargains out there. This month's delivery is 100 grams each of an Ilam spring green from Nepal, a Chota Tingra from Assam, an Upper Namring green from a superb Darjeeling estate, a classic big Halmari Assam and an offbeat Murphalani one.

Five teas, all pedigree and top grade. All unusual and very different from each other, which is the point of the purchase. The 500 grams translates to 17.5 ounces. The price is $60.95, with free shipping, almost exactly 30 cents a cup.

If you decide to try out new teas, get free of the price myth. Your tea will cost you whatever you want to pay for it. The 500 grams of the five Himalayan teas are terrific teas. *And* they are inexpensive. 500 grams of pedigree white teas would be terificer, if there is such a word. And they would be more expensive. Your choice.

Myth 3. Tea bags are as good as loose whole leaf

Tea bags make for uninteresting teas. These are not necessarily bad ones. Not necessarily. In practice, they are a compromise that leads to (1) convenience for the consumer, (2) branding opportunities for the major packagers, (3) streamlined logistics and cost optimization, (4) advantages of scale and automation for growers, wholesalers and distributors, and (5) reliability and standardization.

If a company wants to add "more" to any of these – more convenient, more iced tea/ready to drink/low caffeine varieties, more volume production – then the lower the quality of tea that it will need. High quality, hand plucked, small batch processed and fresh leaf don't contribute to these "mores."

There are moves underway among specialty tea brands to start from the quality end and look for ways to offer really first rate tea, without compromise. That means getting away from the bag of today and using materials, pouches and shapes that get closer to how loose tea infuses in hot water. These are expensive in comparative terms: $1 a bag and on up. It may well be that the combination of quality and convenience will build a specialty market, especially if the teas are fresh and pedigree. Perhaps.

Today's tea bag production is marked by efficiency and consistency. It's as streamlined as the mass manufacturing of, say, plastic cutlery or ball point pens. Pour in the tea at the top of the machine and out comes a flow of blended, labeled, flavored bags. They move down the standard production assembly line to be boxed and made ready for shipment.

One plant produces one of the highest-selling "English" teas in the world: 1.2 million bags *per hour*, a total of 6 billion a year. It's located in Dubai, where it is ideally positioned to optimize bulk ingredient shipping from Africa and Asia. It has used its scale and technology to cut emission wastes from 450 metric tonnes a year to zero, saving 30 thousand square meters of landfill. It exploits all the skills of Agribusiness.

These standards of production, cost, speed and volume explain why the tea bag is both the dominant factor in what gets into the store and the major force in the creeping mediocrity of what the buyer sees. What a supermarket wants on the shelf is a fast-moving, high volume product, with a strong brand and effective marketing, from a reliable supplier, at a competitive cost. These machines make sure they get it;

they do just about everything.

Pour the tea, flavorings and fillers in at the top
Branded custom finished boxes of bags come out on left side tray

Loose leaf tea can't meet these "everything" priorities. This is basically an issue of chemistry and technology. The barrier between the tea and the water in which it is dunked changes the possible reactions. The standard material – a you-don't-really-want-to-know combination of varying grades of cellulose paperish stuff and food quality plastic – doesn't give the leaf space to expand.

High grade whole leaf contents are then literally a waste. Low quality dust is ideal. It gets packaged with variants of this standard lyrical threnody: "We blend tender leaves selected from the best gardens. We then individually wrap our teas in flavor-protecting pouches to seal in its goodness." Sure. You can see the individualization in these machines, and the tender handling.

The tea in the bag is as far away from whole and flavorful by the time it's been through the CTC rotorvanes or green tea heaters. The bag contents all look the same in texture; the differences in flavor often come from additives. One of the images below is actually wood sawdust. It's indistinguishable from the others and can be made to taste like them with any standard food grade extract.

As the original leaf passes through the processing it loses

differentiation. That can be added only through flavorings.

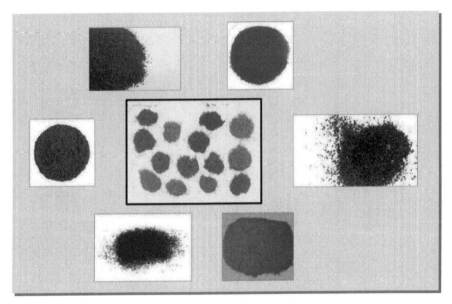

Green, Earl Grey, black, herbal, iced, spice, fruit, chai teas and sawdust

Just a glance at pictures of whole leaf tea variety and tea bag homogeneity makes the visual differences obvious. But they go beyond the superficial. The whole leaf is tea only, sometimes with layered in floral buds and petals. The bags are whatever; the name may be very different from the ingredients. Many are more tea-ish, tea-like or tea-plus something. This is a general issue with food products. What you assume you are getting on a commonsense basis can be disconcertingly less attractive beneath the marketing disguise.

If you buy shredded Parmesan cheese, for instance, you assume that it's cheese. If it is advertised as "added natural fiber", you are likely to see that as a positive contribution to health. In practice, this "cheese" contains cellulose, which sounds OK-ish, in the form of powdered wood pulp – which doesn't quite have the same resonance; but it is "natural." Depending on its exact FDA required classification (pasteurized, spread, prepared or cheese "food"), it may contain less than 51% of what ordinary people would regard as cheese ("optional dairy equivalents").

Welcome to "tea" blends in a bag.

There's nothing "wrong" with the teas below, but there's not much "right" either. They take a proven and entirely natural ingredient, the tea leaf, and add extras to it that in no way improve its taste. The "natural" flavorings are misnamed and largely overpower the tea flavors. The emulsifiers and starches are there only to make manufacturing easier.

All these teas are marketed as natural, healthy and just "tea"

Many tea drinkers will say that they really like their regular teabag choice. Great, so why not try a comparable whole leaf? It will taste better. If you're paying around $5 for a box of bags, there are many better deals for the same price. If you rate your daily drink in a bag as good, the response is the same; here's something better for you in terms of flavor, subtlety, fullness, aroma, "mouthfill" and aftertaste.

The disdain for teabags among experts is often seen as snobbery. It really isn't. The differences between even the best Agribusiness tea bags and an average Artisan whole leaf are very marked. The only reason for sticking with tea bags is convenience and even that is questionable; a simple basket infuser is no messier.

Myth 4. Green tea prevents and cures illnesses

No, it doesn't. Nor does it make you lose weight. The general evidence is that tea is very probably good for your health but there is as yet no reliable proof of its curative or preventive powers.

Scientific research: Here, the record is mildly suggestive but not supportive of claims of specific benefits. The topic is widely researched and there's a broad consensus among scientists that the antioxidants in tea help protect cells and marshal the body's defenses.

But the conclusions are invariably littered with "may", "suggests", "potentially" and the invariable coda of "More research is needed to..." They add up to an unequivocally tentative, preliminary, conditionally definite, qualified "maybe" (possibly) finding about the link (potential) between tea and XYZ – cold cures, cancer prevention, blood pressure, diabetes, depression, weight reduction, ulcer treatment and improved liver functioning.

There is as yet no definitive claim that passes basic tests of statistical reliability, replication, predictive validity, or generalizable results. It's not enough to point to a small sample study that found drinkers of green tea over a few months or in a limited sample showed a weight loss of X or a Y percent lower cancer rate. At most, these are promising but any assertion that they prove the claim is wishful thinking.

Medical practitioners: Opinions among physicians and regulatory agencies vary widely. Some medically licensed doctors, nutritionists, gym trainers, etc., are committed to its playing a key role in their "wellness" programs. The FDA is very clear on its position, which is that there is no support for the health benefit claims. There is not even one instance of any tea-based medication or regime receiving any approval for advertising, prescription and adoption.

In addition, many analysts draw attention to the health *risks*, especially from supplements that contain extracts of green tea.

Tea industry marketing: This is an area of massive misinformation: ignore it all. The ads for green teas, marketed for their anti-oxidants, polyphenols and low caffeine. use scientific language with assertions about cause and effect tea-health links that are unsupported.

The image below is far too typical. It all sounds so positive and so confident. Green tea mythology has built a bandwagon whose drumbeating claims and clamor overwhelm commonsense. There are sixteen bullet point assertions. Pick any three of them. Can you think of a single medicine that treats them all? Two of them? Has your doctor ever prescribed green tea for any of these ailments for you or your family? Does your health insurance cover green tea?

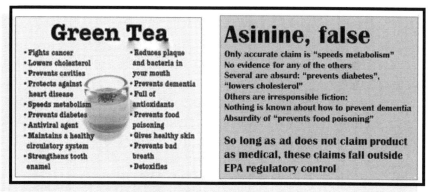

The claims on the left come from a single ad: false and typical. There is no known way to prevent, slow or cure dementia. Nothing "prevents" food poisoning.

This is all arrant nonsense and much of it highly irresponsible, especially "prevents dementia" and "prevents food poisoning." One of the major concerns of modern medicine is that there is not yet even a hint of understanding the dynamics of dementia. Irresponsible may be too kind a term for this so frequent overclaiming of tea as medical magic: shameful seems more accurate.

The FDA periodically issues letters disavowing what is termed "qualified health claims" and periodically sellers and consortia try to get them overturned. (First Amendment are more their base for appeal than any scientific data.)

Tea and you: a tale of 8,000 compounds

At times, discussions of tea seem most like a medical report or a science test. Here's a step back from the details to the broader issue of You, not the tea. If catechins or ECGC are the solution, what is the problem? It's that you are an oxygen-dependent animal in a world where every aspect of your life is affected by other oxygen-dependent, creating, or threatening organisms.

For instance, you rust (more antioxidants, please); your skin gets dry, free radical molecules attack your biological cells and the nutrients you take keep your body in balance (bring in more flavonoids). You move through many stages of growth and health, metabolizing, digesting, absorbing, storing and excreting solids and liquids (more polyphenols, please).

So, think of that cup of tea as one subset of your relationship with oxygen. What makes tea special is that it is the food that has the largest variety and concentration of classes of naturally occurring, versus synthetic, chemical compounds that seem most relevant to making that relationship a good one. In the 1990s, scientists discovered that polyphenols showed signs of being effective in addressing the rust analogy; they are antioxidants.

In addition, they found that particular fruits and vegetables had differing compositions and balance among flavonoids. These classes of polyphenol showed indications, often small and hard to confirm, of beneficial impact on the body's handling of unhealthy oxidants.

The researchers' initial work led to a focus in public policy on a healthy diet which included plenty of fruit and vegetables. This is reflected in the definition of the food pyramid. Tea attracted more and more attention. A new field of chemistry nutrition began experiments, surveys and product innovations based on teasing out the details of the potential – and sellable – links between specific teas and specific illnesses and specific impacts.

The analogy with rusting is a useful one. The human biological system is ever-active. It gets its nourishment from other biological systems that are all a turmoil of chemical ferment. The body has two trillion cells. All the oxidants must be kept in balance. One early indicator of the power of agents that use antioxidants to do so was Vitamin C, long suspected as a solution to the problems of scurvy, the disease that wiped out entire crews of sailors through lack of fresh fruit and vegetables. The synthesis of ascorbic acid after hundreds of years of trial-and-error treatments and studies transformed daily life.

Vitamin C is one of the main antioxidants, along with A and E. Green tea is seen by many as a potential equivalent of Vitamin C. Just as rust attacks a metal, the dark side of the dynamics of oxygen and life is hungry cells. What are termed "free radicals" carry an extra electron. They scavenge the body looking for other cells to attack and start a chain reaction that strips them of their molecules and damages the healthy cells of which they are a part and a support.

The radicals are exogenous; they come from outside and cannot be processed by the body's established biological mechanisms. They include cigarette smoke, pesticides and metals. They are the poisons that can create cancer.

The science of chemistry nutrition zeroed in on antioxidants, starting from the evidence that suggested – note the caution – that they systematically and systemically offered many beneficial impacts on preventing and repairing cell damage. Polyphenols were a widely available source: over 8,000 known compounds that occur in natural form, mainly in fresh fruits and vegetables. Among the most active are flavonoids, 6,000 or so compounds that include the catechins that seem most promising as supplements and health aids. Tea contains the highest concentration of flavonoids. Catechins comprise 25% of the weight of dry green tea leaf. Americans get half of their healthy flavonoids from tea and coffee.

So, that's the story behind the pitch about green tea as a cure for everything. That's far too simple. At most, some combination of some subset of 4,000 flavonols among 6,000 flavonoids among 8,000 polyphenols may have a positive impact on some aspect of your body's chemistry. That impact may be affected by interactions with other active compounds, what's termed bioavailability: how much of the compound in the food is processed by your digestive system, your genetic makeup and many other factors.

All these dynamics are highly situational and interdependent and work at micro levels. Recent research shows that antioxidants can have their own negative effects, overstressing the body's systems. Herbs and medications that are healthy in themselves can be deadly in combination with tea compounds. The various types of tea have very differing different molecular composition: black teas have 80 units of the theaflavins that are believed to inhibit HIV-1 cell replication versus 10 in green teas and none in oolongs.

By contrast, greens are packed with 130 units of catechins and blacks have just 30. Adding milk to black tea doesn't change the tea but eases the microvessels in your blood stream so that they do not process some saporins (immunotoxins inducing cell death by apoptosis; take that, you free radical!).

So, that's the story of the search for the magic tea potion. "It's proven..." No, it's not, but there are still plenty of good reasons to believe. "More research is needed..." Sure, but the progress is encouraging.

The links between tea and health are obviously very complex. They are reviewed in more detail in a separate section. The *Tea Tips* advice is the same whether you feel that tea is good for your health or just that it is good. Buy the tea you like. If it tastes good and there really are benefits, then you get the best of both features. If the benefits are minor or fictional, you still get a good drink. If you buy a tea you don't like only because of the medicinal claims – and the supermarkets and health stores have them in acrid abundance – all you get is a lousy drink. Buy a good one instead.

Myth 5. English tea is special

There is no such thing as English tea. It doesn't exist. Many of the old English companies are now foreign-owned and have shifted their operations far, far away from Shakespeare's "This royal throne of kings, this scepter'd isle." Tea only arrived in England forty years after Shakespeare's death, so at least there can no claim of his drinking tea to correspond with the fairy tales about Earl Grey inventing his tea.

That last sentence needs a modification, alas. Fake English tea labeling is fact-independent. So yes, you can indeed buy Shakespeare's personal tea. "This is his true blend," referenced in Act IV of The Winter's Tale." The actual quote is just "Here's flowers for you, hot lavender, peppermint, summer savory and Earl Grey." The Early Grey mention is not actual; it's a *Tea Tips* add-on, but why not? You can get Tudor Earl Grey and even Ann Boleyn tea; the Tudor dynasty, including Anne, was dead and gone fifty years before the first chest of tea was landed in Europe.

Today, the leading English Earl Grey is processed in Central Europe, the largest brand of English tea is almost all blended and packed in the Middle East, where the ingredients are transported by ship from up to thirty countries. English Breakfast is made in New Orleans with the tea never touching the borders of England. The second largest English tea firm is an Indian company.

The quality of these firms' teas is purely a function of their organization and capabilities. They all source very much the same leaf from the same regions. They process, market and sell them in the same way. There is no aspect of their operations where "English" is meaningful today. The pseudohistory marketing and aristocratic names are vapid claptrap. Never pay extra for any tea because of something in the selling is English Heritage. This statement needs perhaps a little modification: never ever, ever.

The British contribution to tea selling rather than just importing came from mainly Scottish pioneers at the growing end and English merchants plus a smaller number of Irish traders and machine inventors. It was immense and globe-spanning.

China created tea cultivation. Britain invented tea retailing. All the names that became leading global brands initially emphasized that their distinctive strength was in sourcing teas, blending and packaging. The notion of English tea is completely absent; they highlighted that their teas came from Japan, Ceylon, and elsewhere.

The modern blends that emerged from the English innovators' expansion largely downplay this. English tea was a skill in blending. That was what built the historical brands. This had immense and largely beneficial social impacts and made tea affordable and reliable.

English tea was a supply chain revolution not a tea renaissance. Over time, the tea took second place. Here are just a few ads from the 19th century that highlight the source of the teas.

Thomas Lipton was a Scottish discount grocer who developed tea plantations in Ceylon. The Tetley family firm stressed its oolong came from Formosa (Taiwan)

The Englishness of all this mainly lives on in the high tea, Royal, Palace and Earl packaging and pitch. Here's one of the more egregious examples. It's sublimely crass.

> "Every May the Queen holds a garden party at Buckingham Palace—A lovely English springtime tradition... Regal cucumber and watercress sandwiches, served on white bread, smoked salmon Scottish pate, delicately scented Earl Grey cakes, and most importantly: Tea...
>
> "Invitees are exotic guests from the far flung reaches of the Empire... The guests rub shoulders with lords, earls, dukes, duchesses and ladies from aristocratic British society... You can see the scene now—the Queen, Prince Philip and the Queen Mother making eye contact and the royal nod of the head to acknowledge one's presence to those unable to personally meet the Royal Family."

Then comes the eulogy for the tea. It is supposedly "one of the most flavorful teas to come from the British Isles" but it never got anywhere near there in the first place. It seems to be a blend sold in bulk from a company in Washington State that mainly imports teas from Sri Lanka.

The whole message has a touch of Monte Python in it. The royal nod of the head at the thousands of exotic guests ("Exotic" means drunk? Out on bail? Avoiding the infamous tabloids?) The now departed Queen Mother, bless her, was more likely to be downing another gin and tonic than sipping delicately at the whatsit. There is no Empire any more. (Handing Hong Kong back to China marked the formal end.) Earl Grey cake? Delicately scented? That's like talking about lightly perfumed jelly doughnuts.

In 2007, there were over a dozen sites on the Web offering this Buck House Special and using *exactly* the same piece of puffery, word for word. It was still around on several sites in 2017, with Prince Andrew substituted for the Queen Mum. The companies that use this stock material took it from a supplier or wherever to tart up their sales pitch. They know nothing about what it says, including the fact that the Queen Mother died in 2002 (at the age of 101).

Just change the name of the tea to, say, Taj Mahal Imperial. Invent a story about this being the special brew that the Mughal Emperor Shah Jahan always drank to relieve his sorrows for the loss of his favorite wife, for whom he built the Taj Mahal as her mausoleum in 1632-1648.

You don't like that one? Well, how about Versailles Palace tea, beloved by Louis the Whichever (you can pick from I to XVIII) and his official maitresse Madame de Quelquelieu? It's the same tea. That Royal Palace Garden Party blend wouldn't change in any way if were labelled O'Hare Airport Black Brew.

This type of marketing draws attention away from the tea itself and ups the price. Here's what's Royal about it: nothing, zilch, nada, rien, niente, zippo. And as for what's English: same comments, but louder.

Myth 6. "Natural" and "organic" are best choices

All tea is "natural." It should naturally be "organic." Alas, these two simple words are not quite what they imply. A tea *labelled* as natural and organic could well be a toxic danger to health and poor in quality. Equally, one listed as just "tea" may be truly natural and organic. To add to the semantic tap dance, "natural tea" is generally not tea but a herbal mix. "Tea" comes from the tea bush, camellia sinsensis, and contains some level of caffeine.

Yes, natural organic tea is what you should want personally and is also desirable socially and environmentally. But these are characteristics of the tea, not adjectives on the label. Herbal and flavored teas can be unnaturally natural in that their additives and flavorings are found in nature, like common food boosters such as wood pulp and soy lecithin are: largely harmless but you really don't want to know how they are made.

They can also naturally poison you. There are more recalls for pesticides, mislabeling and risks from the herbal equivalent of drug interactions than for any naturally natural teas. A typical alert (2016) is that from the American Heart Association that natural cold remedies, herbal compounds and green tea extracts pose a significant danger to patients, including weakening their heart muscles and increasing sodium and fluid retention.

One significant problem is that the most natural of teas can have unnatural impacts. Many green tea diet aids are in supplement form. The FDA does not have any authority to inspect these before they enter the market or to monitor them. They are brought in only after something bad is reported. That happens too often, alas.

Here's a summary from *Consumer Reports* of a panel of physicians and researchers listing GTE (green tea extract) as one of 15 potentially harmful supplements: risks include "dizziness, ringing in the ears, reduced absorption of iron; exacerbates anemia and glaucoma; elevates blood pressure and heart rate; liver damage; possible death."

Yes, but it's all natural so it's good for you. Really?

"Organic" is more meaningful. The problem is that the label costs time and money to obtain, with a complex certification process and frequently large fees. It also doesn't address the nature of the tea itself, only that it is free of pesticides, chemical fertilizers and practices that threaten the environment and sustainable farming. It excludes from the organic rating levels of lead, high caffeine, low antioxidants and sugar.

This comment about the process in India applies word for word to China, Sri Lanka and Kenya, with the four nations adding up to 90% of global exports:

"The cost of obtaining an organic certification for its tea estate becomes prohibitive which is the reason most of the small tea growers in Assam have not been able to obtain the organic certification for their tea estates yet, despite following organic tea cultivation practices since the beginning. Moreover, the time taken to receive the final organic certificate is three years, which is a very long period."

Many experts comment that the quality of the teas produced by the 800 small growers in Kenya is substantially much higher than that of the large agencies, that have the advantage in the global market of the "organic" cachet.

Pesticides are a growing concern with teas, as with all agricultural products. The organic label screens out this problem. In general, imported teas seem reasonably safe. Japan and the European Union have very tight regulatory standards and while the rules for labelling in the US are not as strict or comprehensive, these two regimes in effect set a global common base for tea quality.

Mountain teas are markedly lower in pesticide use than lowland farms, though not as much as growers claim. The voracious appetite of bugs plus the increasingly disruptive changes in climate patterns make some use of pesticides almost inevitable. Most are harmless and only ones that are water soluble pose a threat, because tea is not cooked and thus the body does not ingest and digest the leaf.

There are many scare stories that are difficult to validate. One area of scariness that can be dismissed, though, is concern about GMO crops: genetically modified organisms. There are no such teas. Evolution and innovation come from clonal methods that do not change the tea but use seedlings and cuttings to select and propagate varieties that have particular characteristics.

So, yes, organic tea should be your preferred choice, and you certainly don't want to buy unnatural tea. But organic is not merely a matter of labeling. It's the full biodynamic fusion: terrain, soil and bush replenishment, and growing and harvesting methods. This is a characteristic of the pedigree of a region, terrain, Artisan harvesting and processing, grower reputation, and tea name identity.

Myth 7. Green teas have the least caffeine

On average, sort of. Well, not really. There is no relationship between darkness and lightness of the leaf and caffeine. Most of the figures on caffeine are averages that were calculated decades ago and are in many instances little more than guesstimates. Green tea does not contain less caffeine than black tea. White tea is not somehow healthier for you than green because it is lower in caffeine. It isn't always lower; some whites are ultrahigh in milligrams per serving.

The scientific consensus is that caffeine evolved as a natural defense system. The bitter taste discouraged insects and creatures looking for a leafy appetizer, by creating a nasty bitter taste. The most vulnerable fresh buds and young leaves of tea bushes generate the highest amounts of caffeine. That's why white tea may contain higher levels than an oolong. Don't accept as a reflex response the fallacy that the darker the tea the higher the caffeine, and conversely the paler its leaf, liquor and lightness of taste, the less the caffeine. Not so.

Here are two first rate teas: one very high in caffeine and the other low: A black China Keemun that is medium-full in taste and a Silver Needle white that is exquisitely delicate and as light as a tea can be without becoming watery in taste.

Silver Needle: white, light, delicate. Keemun, black, full, robust

The image of the two teas is a sort of Rorschach test: what jumps out as the higher in caffeine? Almost certainly, the reaction is the darker one. But it's the *white* tea that's caffeine-packed. It's three times higher in milligrams per cup than the black Keemun. That reflects the springtime freshness and fullness of the buds plucked from the very tip of the bush, with none of the lower leaf selected.

Caffeine: a short briefing

Here's the standard chart of average levels of caffeine. It is not as reliable as it appears. Averages don't cover range. The average height of women is: USA 5'4", India 5'0", China 5'2", Nepal 4'11", and the Netherlands 5'7." Try making, say, a one-size fits all pants suit. Black tea caffeine averages 40 milligrams; the range is 15-110. Green averages 20, from 15-45. The table is just an approximation.

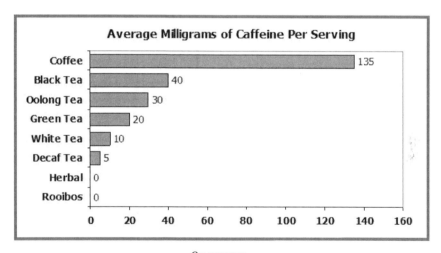

On average...

The scientific consensus is that a daily intake of up to 300 milligrams has no negative medical impacts, except for people at risk from heart problems, pregnant women and nursing mothers, and anyone subject to hypertension. Caffeine consumption in the US is below 250 mg for all age groups.

Tea has around a third the caffeine per cup of coffee: 20-60 milligrams versus 60-120 for most of the ones you will routinely drink. Coca-Cola and Pepsi are 40 milligrams. (The self-proclaimed highest caffeinated drink in the world is Death Wish coffee, which contains 660 mg per 12 oz cup.)

From a medical perspective, caffeine in tea is thus not a danger *for most people*; you can drink ten to twenty cups a day before you hit the recommended and conservative limit of 400 milligrams; the Mayo Clinic identifies 500-600 mg as the safe maximum. However, physicians warn that a constant intake of this amount can – not will – pose kidney and liver problems.

"Most" people doesn't mean all, of course, but the scare mythologies about caffeine make it sound far more dangerous than it is. The general rule of thumb is that 3-4 cups of coffee add up to the daily safe caffeine dose. How about four cups of tea instead, maybe a morning black sensibly brewed for 3-4 minutes (30 mg), a mid-morning oolong (30 mg on average), an afternoon green (20 mg) and mid-evening take your pick (say, 20 mg)? That's 100 milligrams.

Myth 8. Most tea comes from China and India

China and India are the world's largest producers of tea, accounting for half the global total, but there are around forty countries growing, consuming and exporting it at a level that makes it an important element of their rural economies. The mass market teas are mainly machine-processed and from Africa, especially Kenya, Malawi and Uganda, from Argentina and from lowlands in Asia, such as Malaysia, Vietnam and Bangladesh.

Almost all the world's finest tea comes from highland regions. China, India, Taiwan, Japan and Sri Lanka are standouts, with bargains and varieties from Nepal, Indonesia and a few small-scale estates in countries that mainly produce teas that even the national tourist board describes as "unexceptional."

While half of the world's tea is *made* in China and India, most of what you *buy* comes from elsewhere. 90% of China's harvest is consumed domestically, for instance, as is Japan's. By contrast, almost all Argentina's production is shipped to the US.

The largest exporter of teas in the world is Kenya. One review mentions, without noting the irony, that it provides the ingredient for most "Indian" teas. Its production is noted for bold, full taste; that's attractive for blending English/Irish/Morning Breakfasts. Malawi is second in export volume to Kenya among the many African producers and a substantial player in the global market; the selling point is the rich red liquor in the cup; this enhances the appearance of otherwise ho-hum blacks in a bag.

The best teas reflect the old cliché about real estate: Location, location, location. Here's a broad summary of the distinctive strengths and weaknesses of the major producer countries that export tea rather than, as with Iran, import and consume almost all of it domestically. They are listed in rough order of volume, with "√√" indicating actively seek out these teas in your search.

China: Inexhaustible variety of outstanding Artisan teas, along with mass farmed commodity leaf. Find a reliable supplier. Best choice in general for green teas. Home of puehrs. Standard-setter for whites. Underrated blacks. √√

India: Best first choice for black teas. Assams: big and filling. Darjeelings: an orchestra of flavor; almost a mini-industry in and itself in terms of range, cachet, harvest ratings, individualized styles. Nilgiris: plain, really pleasing, many excellent buys. √√

Kenya: Little of distinction. Largest exporter, robust ingredient for English Breakfast style tea bags. Very much the price setter in the global market.

Sri Lanka: Known as Ceylon teas (old colonial name). Some stunning black teas, in the same league as Darjeelings. Full and smooth. Excellent whites. √√

Vietnam: Avoid; mostly bitter greens sold with health pitch.

Turkey: Mostly domestic consumption. Fine mint teas.

Indonesia: Several distinctive blacks, so-so overall.

Argentina: Avoid. Lowest end machine mulch for iced teas.

Japan: Stunning greens, limited exports. High priced. √√

Thailand: Bulk green, mediocre.

Bangladesh: Tea bag filler.

Malawi: Tea bag basic, known for rich color of liquor that makes it look better than it is.

Korea: Avoid green tea bags. Awful is too kind a label.
Taiwan: Becoming the very best for oolongs. √√
Nepal: Fast-developing, many of the best bargains. √√

Myth 9. You can store tea in the fridge

The simplest way to wreck a good tea is to do nothing and just stick it anywhere. It is hard to exaggerate just how dynamic and absorbent tea is. That is the very basis for flavored teas like Earl Grey or the much subtler jasmine greens. There, the odors are delicate aromatics, but teas absorb onion smells as readily as lavender.

The rules for storing tea are simple but absolute: no light, heat or air. Follow them and your tea will keep fresh and full of flavor for a good six months and even a year. Tea absorbs just about anything in the air, especially moisture, heat and aromas. That makes the refrigerator one of the worst places to store it. Along with placing it next to the kitchen stove, in a glass jar, or a loose semi-open packet.

At your end, storage is simple but vital. Tins. With tight lids. A dark shelf away from heat. Pick from among the many bright and functional designs available in any tea outlet.

Functional storage priority: tight-fitting lids. Design options: plain to fancy.

Myth 10 Tea is best with milk and sugar

Tea and sugar have always been a pair, outside the Chinese and

Japanese tradition. Milk similarly was historically very much part of European black tea consumption. It's a personal choice and to some extent a national social habit. In general, the better the tea, the less the need for milk and sugar. The *Tea Tips* recommendation is that if you do use them, try drinking your tea neat. It's likely that you'll start cutting back as you try out lighter and more aromatic teas, but it's no big deal. Just enjoy your drink.

The addition of milk is obviously linked to black tea. The stronger and rougher the tea the more the need to soften it. In cold climates, tea was very much a filling source of nutrition, and dairy cultures naturally boosted the drink with milk. This was most marked in Ireland, which ranks as one of the two countries with the highest tea consumption per capita.

In general, US preferences are for slightly softer black teas. The English Breakfast marketed by the global brands is a lighter and flatter blend for the US market, for instance. Irish tea by contrast is in the paint-stripper class: big Assams and Rwanda blends – and lots of milk. The shift in English tea from Chinese imports to ones from Assam and Ceylon in the mid to late 19tth century greatly increased both the fullness and often the roughness of tea. Milk took a central place.

India's adaptation of the colonial harvest to its own culture, marsala chai, combined lower grade heavy tea with milk as the base for spices and sweeteners. In Russia and Mongolia, two major black tea cultures, milk was added to the tea to make it easier to digest and enrich its food value.

There's a cost to these benefits. Adding milk doesn't seem to affect the tea itself – whether you put the milk in first or after the tea is poured. (This quasi-theological point was for long a matter of serious debate. The evidence suggests that the social norm was to pour it in first to protect the fragile bone porcelain from cracking from a jolt of boiling tea. Maybe.)

Milk does inhibit the body's absorption of polyphenols. It also affects digestion. Tea relaxes blood vessels, tea with milk doesn't. Many experts argue that the vascular benefits of tea are both substantive and lost if milk is added. The main final argument against milk is that it alters your sense of taste when drinking lighter teas. You lose some of the wonderful subtleties and overtones of Darjeeling and China Keemun and Yunnan teas.

All in all, there is no reason to add milk to your tea and several reasons not to. But it is of minor concern and you should decide based on personal enjoyment. It's worth checking though if you include milk as habit rather than choice; try going without it for a few cups.

Sugar is a much more complex issue. Again, it is very much linked to national tea cultures. In some, especially Turkey, the highest per capita consumer nation, Morocco and Iran, tea is carefully sweetened with sugar or honey. Cakes and candies are routine accompaniments in many societies. Rock sugar is a tea staple in Germany. Many Indian chais are sugar-loaded. English tea used to be an accompaniment to swiss rolls, chocolate digestive bikkies, jam sarnies and gateaux.

But sugar was never part of China's tea culture, going back to the 8th century. Nor was it prevalent in Europe's first century of tea imports and expansion, outside England, where sugar was already a growing staple. Elizabeth I's strong diplomatic relationships with Turkey gave England trade agreements that were not open to the Catholic nations the alliance was formed to oppose. There's a case to be made that sugar fueled the acceleration of tea and vice versa, and that this partly accounts for why the rest of Europe did not adopt tea as its norm.

Part of the reason for the addition was that tea is naturally astringent and sugar provides an offsetting sweetness. But it was far more driven by one simple factor: addiction. Sugar became something people couldn't do without. It dominates the 17th and 18th century history of trade, colonialism, slavery, politics and agriculture.

The issue for tea drinkers is should they now do without it in general, and can they? The health risks are well-known and growing in severity.

Here are some figures from a thorough research study by the respected Euromonitor. The average daily consumption of sugar per capita in the US is around 120 grams (2015). Germany is second at 100. The World Health Organization's recommendation is 50 grams per day, making the US two and a half times above the comfortable limit.

The lowest figure is India at 10 gms, with most Asia countries below 30. The bottom three countries have an obesity rate of about 2%. The US one is 35%. The question is not should you add sugar to your tea but should you add sugar?

Summary: Demythologizing tea: quality and value

All these myths and misconceptions lead to paying too much for not very good bags and blends, brewing them for too long and at the wrong temperature and being misled by marketing myths and hype.

More consequentially, they easily box you into a very constrained view of value *to you*: what to consider in terms of taste, variety, price, aroma, caffeine, healthiness, freshness, smoothness, sweetness and overall satisfaction.

The myths are presented together in *Tea Tips* to provide a broad picture of the tea scene as perceived by many people who, reasonably enough, don't know what they don't know about tea and in most instances, have no interest in finding out much about it.

Clearing away the myths points towards a very different picture that doesn't require much effort or expertise to provide a more accurate focus. It is not so much about tea but choosing tea and getting enjoyment and value from it. The myths encourage mediocre and even rotten choices

Tea Tips expands on the topics raised in the discussions of the Ten Tea Myths in later individual sections. Once you dismiss them, there are so many choices.

Growing tea: Location, Craft and Climate

The tea bush

There's a hoary adage that money doesn't grow on trees. With tea, it really does, on just a single plant, the *camellia sinensis*.

All tea, however different, starts from this bush.

Tea farming began in China, though there was fragmented harvesting of the wild plant in India five thousand years ago, for medicinal use as a pounded herb rather than a drink. The official sounding mythical start in Chinese history is pinpointed as 2732 BCE (probably a Thursday.) Maybe a better dating is Star War's vague opening of "A long time ago in a galaxy far, far away...", except that in this instance it's on a mountain.

Regardless, camellia sinensis has been harvested for a recorded 3-4,000 years. There's a remarkable degree of continuity in the core of the Artisan craft. Even today, there are many elements that are in essence the same: the manual methods of harvesting, the recipes for creating a green versus black, puehr or oolong, the ceremony and rituals, clay-based pots and cups – and the bush.

3,000 years ago   *2,000*   *No*

That said, the main direction of tea making and selling is now away from craft towards an industrial manufacturing process. In a world of technology, mass production, globalization and consumerization, most of the Artisan core has been transformed.

But not the bush. Through all these past stages and for the coming era, it remains genetically the same, though evolving extra characteristics through hybridization and clonal seedlings. There's no different plant for black teas, greens, oolongs, puehrs or whites. Tea bags, blends, iced tea, whole leaf, Imperial Grade plucking and CTC are different in how the leaf that gets to your cup is harvested, processed and packaged (and flavored or added to), but it's all from the same two varieties of the camellia sinensis bush: *var. Sinsensis* and *var. Assamica.*

The image below shows the two varieties side by side, with pictures from across the world of the hand harvesting that selects and plucks the best leaf. They are the global foundation of tea cultivation.

Assam plant   China plant

Sinensis: The China bush. Assamica: Indian

Very roughly, Sinensis dominates green tea production and Assamica is the base for the black tea industry. The name muddle of sinsensis Sinensis – Chinese Chinese – and sinsensis Assamica – Chinese Indian, reflects the assumption of just a single bush variety. Among botanists, traders and explorers. "Tea" meant "Chinese."

Sinensis is the Chinese bush that for thousands of years was assumed to be the only tea plant. Assamica is the Indian variety first discovered growing wild in Assam, India, in the 1830s. Any beverage made from the harvest of one of these two varietals or the various hybrids that have been evolved counts as tea. Nothing else does.

Many herbal drinks are "tea" but that is like calling soda a sweet wine. Roobois is popular as one of these sorta kinda teas; it comes from the South African honeybush and is caffeine-free. In Latin America, tea never became popular and the main nonalcoholic beverages are coffee and yerba mate, a caffeine-rich leaf mixture drink from the rainforest holly tree.

Each type of true tea leaf reflects the climate and terrain that it evolved in and which led to the main division in tea production and consumption over the 19th and 20th centuries. The English tea culture became more and more built on heavy black teas, and Assamica was spread across British colonies, most notably Ceylon, now known by its post-independence name of Sri Lanka. The dominance of China eroded in the global market, and today most of its production is for domestic consumption, as is the case in Japan.

The Assam bush is less tolerant of temperature extremes and requires plenty of rain and drainage. Its leaves can grow to nine inches in length. It is fundamentally the cultivar ("cultivated variety") for producing a malty and robust base for processing, with the China leaf lighter and more vegetal.

Regardless of the exact variety of the bush and the tea it results in, the single iconic symbol is the tip of the bush: the two leaves and a bud that in effect define the Artisan tradition. In general, this is the best: best in terms of nutrients, freshness, chemical compounds, flavors, aromas, smoothness, and opportunities for creating a distinctive tea.

The lower the harvester moves down the branch – a machine, shears or plucker's hand – the less fine the tea will be. That's not an absolute. While the very best white teas are made only of buds that are completely fresh and harvested just once a year in a time window of a few weeks, some oolongs are from more mature leaf and the best puehrs use much more of the bush.

That said, machine- versus hand-plucked harvesting – the very first stage of processing – sets the limits or opportunities for all the rest: very same bush, very different tea taste and complexity. More consequentially: the same name the tea can be sold as.

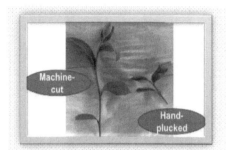

The buds and top leaf are where the nutrients concentrate the flavor compound.
A machine collects 5-8 times the sellable harvest per bush/acre

The extent of the variations among the individual teas each produces is marked with both Sinensis and Assamica. Japanese green teas are an example: a unique side road from the main paths, in terms of style, growing, processing and brewing. They are from the same Sinensis bush as China's teas but are steamed. This preserves the natural enzymes and softens the leaf, giving it a darker green color and vegetal taste.

Japanese Sinensis is used for unique combinations. Genmaicha adds toasted rice. Kukicha is roasted twigs, matcha the much-prized powder tea central to the Japanese tea ceremony.

The terraced hill in Japan shown above could be a green tea garden in China, Korea or Vietnam but the nine teas shown alongside the image are uniquely Japanese. Their differences from the mainstream and among each other come from subtle variations in processing, including Kukicha breaking all the two leaves and a bud rules to turn twigs, stems and stalks into a smoky, smooth and ever so slightly sweet delight.

A quick digression... One of the pleasures and sometimes con games with teas is that there's always a Legend for the ads. Take your pick from these three for genmaicha, the pleasant tea with added popped rice:

Samurai: 15th century, servant accidently drops a few grains of roasted rice he'd stuck up his sleeve for later snack into his warlord's tea. Samurai not pleased, applied the standard fine, equivalent to $100 for speeding. Well, actually samurai beheads servant – same thing – sits back down, tries it, loves it. Terribly sorry. Names it after now very dead servant,

Buddhist lore: Medieval monks scraped rice from the bottom of their cauldrons and added green tea as "a gesture of humility or conservation." (Really?) That comes from one of the very best tea brand's ads; it earns marks for imagination.

Crass commerce: Housewives had long added rice to the lowest quality bancha, which had a reputation as an awful tea. A Tokyo tea seller had the smart idea in the 1920s of using higher grade sencha. He thought of naming it Daimyo – Warlord – a meaningless attribution, like Erlgraycha.

Different legends: same tea. Different teas: same bush.

And then there are puehrs. These are also from the Sinensis bush, just like the Japanese teas. The Japanese variety produces small leaves in tidily trimmed and laid out rows. Puehrs include wild bushes that are permitted to grow into trees with extra-large leaves. Many of these are claimed to be one to two thousand years old.

Puehrs are by far the most complex of teas. They are unique in that their bacteria continue to ferment over many years – fifteen is still "young" – and there are ones that are over a century old. They are wide ranging in flavors, with descriptors like earthy, damp and mushroomy.

They come in many forms: compressed brick, bowl, "raw" and "cooked", tuocha, melon and pressed inside an orange or bamboo stem. Both China puehr bing cakes and Japanese sencha are the same in ingredient, with nothing added to the Sinsensis leaf. That they look and taste so different is the result of nothing more than timing, air and heat.

All these puehrs come from the Sinensis bush left to grow to a tree and not kept pruned

There are new varieties of leaf emerging from research and investigation of cloning techniques along with Sinensis-Assamica hybrids. Their impact is spreading. The AV2 clonal, for example, is the base for some of the highest rated Darjeeling black and newer white teas. Others are improving resistance to mold, reducing water usage, providing faster growth and protecting against heat changes. Japan's entire industry is built on a combination of clonals developed over many decades.

Japanese teas are almost all clonal. They were a systematic response in the 1970s to a surge in demand for green tea hampered by shortages of land and workers. The industry looked to mechanize without losing quality and create a varietal that had high yield and well-formed buds.

The Yabukita clonal was a superb solution. It was very upright in its growth as opposed to spreading and its leaves were an intense shiny green that provided a novel new taste – "umami" meaning sweetness – that has become a hallmark of Japanese teas. It spread across the market, accounting for over three quarters of all tea.

That led to the standard nature fights back scenario: overreliance on a monoculture plant, outbreaks of plant pests and diseases and overproduction. Clonal development shifted to adding diversification and formal testing of new cultivars. Yabukita remains the dominant variety but there are now eight main ones in established use and around fifty registered for application.

Asatsuyu
Early cultivar, mother of many others
Early season maturation
Small buds, highly fragrant tea
Astringent

Yabukita
High yield, bold taste
Heavy fertilizer needs
Hardy growth
Vulnerable to grey blight disease

Okumudori
Later maturation, extends
harvesting season
Grows and spreads fast

Japanese clonal Sinensis are natural selections from seedlings,
chosen to give a Darwinian nudge to evolve the species

Clonals illustrate the problem and the solution for tea growing. The tea can only be as good as the bush. The problems include climate threats, erosion of the soil and environment, and underinvestment in replacing low-yield plants. Clonal development is an answer to all three of these. It will be a central force in innovation.

Kenya has even propagated a bright purple clonal leaf, high in anthocyanins, an antioxidant with possible health benefits and proven uses as a food coloring.

Kenya's purple TRFK 315 clonal commands a price four times that for Kenyan black tea.

The tea is marketed as "plummy" and "powerful"; "coruscating" may be more accurate. Purple tea has transformed the livelihoods of small Artisan growers, who have been under continuing pressures from falling export prices. It sells for four times the commodity crop.

Tea farms and gardens

Left in its natural state, the bush will flower, just like decorative camellias. It can grow as high as 80 feet and live for well over 100 years. Here's the spectrum of groomed versus untamed bush, and field versus wilderness location.

Korea green tea farm   *China mountain oolong*   *Sri Lanka estate*

Tea farms plant the bushes in rows and keep them at just over a meter and shaped into a rounded tabletop form, to make it easy to pluck. A bush has a productive life of, typically, 60 years. Mountain estates let it sprawl more so that the fields are patches of bush rather than tidy lines. In a few instances, as in the middle image, the plants grow wild and there is no effort to tame and tide them up. The terrain very much determines the farming options.

The two images below entertainingly capture the extremes of selectivity, delicacy and destination of the harvest. The first epitomizes two-leaves-and-a-bud and shows workers plucking leaf for one of the world's great, marvelous, stunning and exquisite oolongs, from the Alishan high mountain region of Taiwan. The other is eight-gears-and-rotating-cutter-blades, a Malaysian monster truck. Lurking in the trees, it looks like it could accommodate a small family. It has its engine, storage, suction, driver controls – and adjustable blades that won't be set to pick off top buds. Anything that grows, goes.

Many hands, light plucking   *30-ft machine chews all its cutters reach*

Malaysia is emblematic of the increasing pressures to switch from Artisan to Agribusiness. Its Cameron Highlands grow high quality teas but the shortage of labor has been too acute for it to establish a strong market presence. The switch from hand plucking to two-person machines increased production from 30 (18 lbs) kilograms of leaf per worker to over 300 kg and reduced the need for traditional skills. Moving down to the lowlands has enabled a behemoth like the one shown to harvest 9 *tons* of leaf a day – 20,000 lbs. This crops the fields faster than new leaf can grow.

The global tea industry has about five brands that account for well over half the market. Size is on their side, for Agribusiness success. 50,000 smallholders in Assam farm an average of under three acres of tea plants. China has an estimated 80 million tea farm workers. The average acreage is a hundredth of that for the state-run farms. But it's the farms that dominate production, distribution and, in the end, economics. They have advantages of scale.

And of licenses. The Chinese government does not permit smallholders to export their produce. That gives oligopolistic control to large companies: farms, factories and wholesalers. Alas, it means that the best of China's teas is rarely obtainable abroad.

This has many impacts along the supply chain, from field to retail outlet. You, the tea drinker, are at the end of this chain. You ought to be in charge of it. In practice, *most shoppers don't have a clue either what they are getting, how it gets to them, or what their choices are.*

Say you want to find a China green tea. What you'd like is the best value in terms of a combination of flavor, price and special characteristics that add to your personal enjoyment. You won't get that value from the large farms that sell in volume to the packagers and global brands.

The China tea that you're interested in is made by hundreds of small farmers; some is mediocre, most goes to the state-run factory and is processed for export and the best is sold locally. So, if you want the very best available, you'll need to buy through a specialist who knows how to deal with the arcane anti-small business export system.

Here's the punchline: since all these come from the same generic bush, *it is easy to claim that the teas are the same.* The highlighted phrase summarizes just about every element of tea marketing, branding, supply chain, packaging and pricing. Make hot dogs; sell steak. You may think you've never bought Malaysian tea. If you drink any of the leading brands' ice teas or "pekoe cut" black tea bags, you definitely have.

The trade press is consistent in admitting that customer ignorance is one of their prime drivers of business strategy here. Obviously, there is no way you can or should even try to know all the details of your tea's farming. You can and should, though, apply the single screening rule below to zero in on the best teas.

Choose a megabrand mountain

Almost every great tea is associated with a mountain or range. Examples are rock oolongs like Big Red Robe and Iron Goddess of Mercy from Wuyi (China), High Mountain oolongs from Alishan (Taiwan), Kanchenjunga black teas, (the third highest mountain the world, better known by the name of the town of Darjeeling), the small farm matcha, sencha and gyokuro greens of Uji (Japan), or Nuwara Eliya black teas (Sri Lanka).

These mountains provide the climate in which tea most thrives: seasonal temperature ranges, elevation, biodiversity, and location in the paths of the rain and wind that feed its soils. They enable specialization of growing and tea making that exploit their localized characteristics and the building of entire cultures and communities that maintain and pass on their skills. (This has long had a dark underside: colonial indentureship and effective serfdom, widespread and increasing poverty, and worker exploitation.)

There are teas where you need to know only the mountain region: it's a megabrand. There will be many individual differences among them, but they provide a solid reference point, as with, say, pedigree French wines. "*Burgundy*, estate-bottled, premier cru, Volnay, 2013; *Darjeeling*, single estate, Rishehaat, first flush, 2016" lays it out.

These four mountains alone produce a wide range of the world's best teas, spanning China, Taiwan, Japan and Sri Lanka:

Wuyi, China	Alishan, Taiwan	Uji, Japan	Nuwara, Eliya
Rock oolongs	*High mountain*	*Sencha*	*Black OP*
Big Red Robe	*Dongding oolong*	*Gyokuro*	*Lover's Leap*
Iron Goddess	*Zhong Shu Hu, Zhi Zuo*	*Matcha*	*Court Lodge*

Here are ten megamountains that produce around 300 individual and very different teas. It is not an exaggeration to say that if you bought the most noted teas from just these megabrand regions, you would have a lifetime of unsurpassable choices.

These mountains produce the black tea Darjeelings of India, China Keemuns and Sri Lanka's Ceylons. Oolongs include China Wuyi Big Red Robe, Iron Goddess of Mercy and Golden Water Turtle, and its Taiwanese rival High Mountain teas, Oriental Beauty and Dongding. Greens are the Mao Fengs of China, Japanese sencha, matcha and Gyokuro, and the whites Moonlights and Silver Needles of India, Sri Lanka and China. Finally, there are the raw and ripe puehrs of China.

Prices for these megamountain teas are higher than average and the top end ones can command the same "$$$$" catalog notation as rare wines. But you can stock up on fine grades of all their main showcase names for 50-60 cents a cup and there's no reason ever to pay more than an average of $1 a cup for the best of the best.

Megabrand	Location	Noted teas
Alishan	Taiwan	High Mountain oolongs: Dong Ding
Darjeeling	India	Black teas of superb quality, variety, character; 90 estates; traditional hand-plucking, processing
Huangshan	China	Some of the very best teas, both black, green and white: Keemun, Mao Feng
Li Shan	Taiwan	Taiwan oolongs are in some instances surpassing the Chinese ones with the same name and style. An immense range of small grower varieties.
Nuwara Eliya, Dimbula, Uva	Sri Lanka	The three highland megabrands of Ceylon tea. In the Darjeeling, elite class with a heavier, fuller style.
Uji	Japan	Near Kyoto, produces many of the best and most subtle Japanese green teas: matcha, sencha, Gyokuro
Wuyi	China	The home of oolongs.
Xishuangbana	China	The region where all the great puehrs are made.

Uncluttering tea descriptions

Megabrands help unclutter the information hyperglut and babble in choosing teas: vacuous puffery at one extreme and tea-talk overload at the other. Teas are difficult to describe and label. It's easy to pick out what makes a bad tea a shock to your nervous system with a shudder or grimace more expressive than words. It's much harder to verbalize and compare a good light China green tea with an equally fine Taiwan oolong.

Tea is very subtle, with its aroma, taste, texture and aftertaste all contributing to the experience. The problem is that accurate descriptions by a tea specialist don't communicate – a description of a tea as "a panorama of flavors, gradient palate profile, tempering sensory experience; mildly mineral-like note" and comparisons that the average tea drinker cannot even relate to: roasted chickpea, green guava and "an elegant attack of stewed papaya." (!). Others are enthusiastic waffle: "Iridescent floral flavors, the top notes are anxious and unrestrained." (Can a flavor be iridescent and anxious?)

These are typical, not outliers, in tea puff.

This level of description is for experts – growers, tea firms' buyers, the very skilled tasters who source teas for the global brands, test a wide range of items on offer, and coordinate the supply from dozens of countries to ensure quality and consistency in their final goods. For them, the difference between, say, a black tea that is geranium, tropical and melon versus another one marked by being decaying wood, mineral and wet rock is marked, whereas your own non-expert response may be "Duh?"

The megabrand simplifies evaluating individual teas without needing such subtleties of discrimination; those can develop to the degree and depth of your own preference. The megabrand mountain identity is enough information to guide your more detailed exploration and assessment. Select one for any style of tea that you are interested in – Chinese or Japanese greens, Indian black tea, oolongs, puehrs, flavored tea, white tea, select a mountain megabrand.

Then just apply a simple rule: *Pick any one of its teas that takes your fancy*. This recommendation is the key one. Don't bother with being systematic. Just browse the description, check the price and hit the "Submit Order" screen option. In the description look for information that gives you what makes this tea a little distinctive or unusual.

You can become more selective as you zero in on the styles of tea you most like and have a comparison base to help you. So, for instance, your discoveries among Darjeeling estates will naturally nudge you to try Ilam Nepalese black and Nilgiris and lowland estate Assams. From Uji senchas, it's equally likely that you'll be tempted to try ones from Kagoshima and the specialized, small farm senchas of Shizuoka. You just need a starting point for expanding to teas that are out of your ordinary space of knowledge and experience.

Take as an example, looking for a good Chinese black tea. There are a hundred or more varieties offered by reliable providers. The choice is wide as is the information: too much so for most shoppers. What's the flavor difference between a Hubei Keemun Ji Hong, An Hui Keemun Xiang Luo, Hao-Ya "A" Superfine Keemun, Hunan Mao

Feng, Keemun Panda #1, and Fujian Panyang Tippy Mao Feng?

Please note that the following summary is intendedly eye glazing. It is packed with information that doesn't really inform. The point it makes is that information is useful only in terms of clarification, orientation and understanding. One of the most irritating aspects of tea literature and advertising is that they assume more information means more understanding. So, here's some uninforming information and disorienting orientation.

The teas above are all similar China "congous." They are terrific. Keemun is one of the best black teas in the world. Xiang Luo translates to "fragrant spiral." Hao-Ya is the highest grade of the Keemun made from leaves plucked just after the first harvest Spring Mao Feng one. Keemun Panda # 1 (Top grade 1) is a bargain for a tea of appealing lightness.

The paragraphs above are not at all helpful. If you were unfamiliar with China black teas before reading them, you probably feel no less so now. But you really should try Chinese congous. They are a smooth and soft complement to big Ceylons and Assams and the more tippy Darjeelings.

So, here's a simple recommendation: Check Huangshan (Yellow Mountains). It is the region in Anhui Province, China, which produces Keemuns and Mao Fengs of stunning quality. As with all the megabrand mountains, the setting is stunning, too.

Note the hotel in the center of the bottom left photo and the cliff walkway in the top row

Grab any Huangshan tea offered by a supplier with a good reputation and poetry-free product descriptions. Check the price for (a) what you are willing to spend, and (b) how close it is to that of other suppliers: too cheap means it's probably a lower grade and too much means, well too much.

Megabrands versus individual tea names

There are other mountain brands, of course, but they are less generic in terms of the teas from their region being uniformly distinctive. For example, Nilgiri's spectacular Blue Mountains produce some top rate teas, from estates like Craigmore, Havukal and Glendale, and Orthodox whole leaf Nilgiri is currently one of the best buys on the market: full, plain and pleasing.

But there's also some sorry stuff. Nilgiri threw away its heritage in the 1990s by chasing the Russian and Iranian markets, where price not quality was the selling point. It is only now recovering its reputation and much of the production is low-cost ingredients for low-quality basic teabags. There are fine Nilgiris but Nilgiri doesn't directly equate to fine.

There are some outstanding lowland teas, too, but the regions are not megabrands. Assam is the closest and, as with Nilgiri, produces some superb teas but overall the standard is falling. Growers are losing position in the global export markets to competitors like Kenya, through poor management, climate and seasonal shifts, cost inefficiency and declining quality.

The best Assams remain outstanding and there are comparable valley teas from Sri Lanka and Japan, but these are individual exceptions. New Vithanakande, for instance, is a non-highland Ceylon tea that is one of the best combinations of quality, taste and price you can find. In general, though, the lowlands are best-suited to high volume production, ease of farming and standardization.

Megabrand mountain teas can be defined by adding "not" to each of these largely economic considerations: They are not well-suited to large-scale production; almost every one of them is acres not square miles in size. They are not easy to farm: small patches of hillside land, with trees, rocks and undergrowth instead of wide open fields.

They are not standardized and reliable products that are the same year after year; a late spring rain, dry period and even daily weather shift can alter the taste of top grade mountain teas. They are not tea bag ready. And there is no way a machine can substitute for the selective hand plucking of the very best buds from the bush, on 40-70 degree slopes. In Darjeeling, 45 degrees counts as nearly flat.

The answer to the question of what makes megabrand mountains special is that they must be. These are crazy places for anyone to set up any type of farm and factory, let alone keep them running for hundreds and even thousands of years. Using the old rules of real estate value being a function of location, location and location, these are one step below slum property. Unless you want to make tea.

Climate

The tea bush tolerates a wide range of seasonal and weather variations, but within clear limits of not too hot or too cold and not the same all year round. The best climates are subtropical, with the longest growing season at the equator, and the plants dormant around 18 degrees of latitude North and South.

That's why tea has never, ever thrived in England: too cold. It was grown for a while in the US, in Georgia, but failed because there was not enough elevation and variation in seasonal temperature. Megabrand mountains are rare across the globe and if bushes from them are transplanted or their seeds grown elsewhere, the tea is nowhere near the same. Here's the tick off checklist for the real estate: Remote locations, Rain, Steep slopes, Acid soil, Biodiversity.

Remote locations: What makes the tea mountains rare is that they must meet requirements of height, slope and wind/air/rain patterns: a lot of rain plus a lot of wind and sun. Tea thrives at elevations between 2,000 and 6,000 feet. That rules out Kansas and conurbations. Available mountain ranges with suitable climate are tall, not well-habited and very remote.

Rain, rain and more rain: Tea bushes need around 60 inches of rain a year. They must have excellent drainage or they become waterlogged. Steep slopes provide for that if and only if the soil is protected and provided with plenty of nutrients. The ecology is fragile.

A major concern of all tea growers today is the disruption of rain patterns. This is accelerating with climate change. In many African lowland farms, it has resulted in sustained droughts. In the mountains, the impact is much more on the delicately timed exploitation of differences in the leaf's tenderness, nutrients and maturation at particular times of the year.

This is best illustrated by the Darjeeling distinction of the first and second flush harvests. Separated by just a few months, they are famously contrasting in basic flavor, distinctive characteristics and production, even though they come from the same estates, bushes and locations.

Steep slopes: There's a whole science of what may flippantly be termed slopery or slopiness. Essentially, it reflects the rule that what goes up must come down and if it comes down in the right amounts then you get flourishing tea plants. "It" is moisture carried by winds that collect it from a remote source and carry it up one face of the mountain. It cools, obviously, and the air dries as the pressure gets lower. The side of mountains that faces the winds gets high rainfall and the leeward side of mountains receives the lighter falls in its drier *rain shadow*. Tea is largely grown on the windward slopes of mountain ranges.

One result of this is that the same megabrand tea grown at 6,000 feet will be lighter and tippier than at 3,000 feet. The Namring estate in Darjeeling distinguishes between its Upper and Lower Namring teas for this reason.

The three megabrands of Sri Lanka's Ceylon teas, Nuwara Eliya, Uva and Dimbula produce subtly different teas in terms of fullness, mellowness, and aroma because of the varied mid- to high-range elevation of the slopes. The whole island is about the size of West Virginia, among the ten smallest states on the US, but these three elevated areas create a wider variety of black leaf tea than the lowlands of the whole of Kenya, the largest exporter of teas. Kenya is bigger than California.

Acidic soil: Teas grow best in slightly acidic soil, with a balance of clay and loam to hold the water particles that feed the bushes. It needs a rich mineral content, with organic matter from the bedrock adding to it. Too much precipitation can leach the soil, and most farms and estates must add fertilizers to ensure nitrogen, phosphorus and lime levels.

Soil management is obviously critical for the health of the bush and a major concern for sustaining tea growing in the long-term. The megamountains are generally in sound health in this regard, though investment is often hampered by lack of financial capital, environmental and climate threats, and weak management.

Creepy critters: Related to soil and climate are pests, which are both the friend and foe of tea growers. They are a foe for the obvious reason that in a humid, steamy and biodiverse environment they devour crops. Tea bushes are juicy and nutritious canapés for many hundreds of different types of insect and creepy crawlies. Crop losses can be sudden and substantial. Even with growing use of pesticides, they average 20%. Left unchecked, they range from 10-55%. A few teas are enhanced by insect chomps.

Biodiversity is vital to tea growing for so many reasons, including the eccentric nature of asexual seed reproduction and nurturing of nutrients. The megabrand mountain communities and many of the leading quality blenders and sellers are increasingly, often belatedly, mobilizing to protect the environment and maintain the symbiotic balance with insects that help the chemical interactions of the leaf.

The era of ecological challenge

The bush is core today to tea growing. Its evolution is critical to tea's future. The agenda is (1) respond to climate change and environmental degradation and (2) achieve sustainable profitability by either increasing productivity and yield when competing in the mainstream commodity market of tea bags and iced tea, or increasing quality and "premiumization" that will command higher prices.

It seems likely that mediocre tea will get worse over the coming years. Many undercapitalized large farms and inefficient small growers will fail in both imperatives of economics and quality. The bushes and their soil have been neglected past the age of easy repair. The lead times for renovation are at least ten years from inception – seedlings or clonal cuttings – to productive harvest, and once in place, the growers must live season to season. The experts' consensual annual rate of bush replacement needed to maintain health and productivity is 2%. It has been around 0.7% globally for many decades.

Fine tea is likely to get better. Tea growing as a localized craft has seen many climate shifts over its two to three thousand years. It is highly adaptive and flexible – its Artisan methods adjust daily to weather in harvesting and processing. Its most highly valued names reflect microclimates where there is opportunity as well as challenge.

The innovators are investing in their bushes by adopting clonal plants that have been selected and nurtured for characteristics that help in response to climate threats and impacts: water use, flavor, hardiness, resistance to the flying zoo of tea leaf munching insects, and molecular chemical interactions. Most of all, the elite growers are harvesting clonal teas that create new elements of quality.

The policy, industry and economic agendas and challenges of climate change are unclear. Its impact has become more and more apparent for years at the local level of tea farmers. Global weirding is here. Now. The monsoons get later and more intense in India, waterlogging the plants and killing them off with root rot. Japanese smallholders are sensitive to the increasing unpredictability of rain patterns. Yunnan growers are seeing shifts in quality and yield in their high-end Artisan-crafted green teas, where as one expert comments, flavors can change from morning to afternoon because of shifts in the concentration of amino acids.

The consensus is that production in East Africa is on track to drop by half by 2050. A long drought in Kenya is estimated to cut crops in 2017 by 30%

In Sri Lanka, there is a sense of crisis. The country is a tea economy. Books and articles published twenty years ago uniformly praise its organization, productivity, quality and variety of tea production. Today's headlines are concerns for its lagging productivity, financial losses on export sales, and eroding position in the global market.

Here's the problem. The bushes have passed their age limit. They are mostly 80 years old, with many over 100 years. They were grown from seedlings and are low-yielding hybrids of Sinensis and Assamica. Growers have not kept up with the evolution to clonal cuttings.

But while the ecological challenge is immense, the solutions are well understood. In Sri Lanka, *all* the most substantial productivity and quality gains have come from the smallholders that have applied them, while the politics-entangled large RPCs – Regional Plantation Companies – are flailing.

Similarly, one the most prestigious names in the world, Darjeeling, fell into disrepute through a comparable post-independence transfer of ownership, overproduction, reliance on chemicals, and an aggressive pursuit of volume at the expense of quality to meet the demands of the Russian market for Indian black teas, but only at low prices.

That market collapsed. So, did much of the landscape. Soil erosion brought landslides and many deaths, Entire estates were abandoned, leaving workers without jobs and the food and housing that had compensated for low wages.

Assam flood in tea growing area   *Darjeeling flood*

Now, the magic is coming back. It's still a long battle but the distinction "organic" is no longer a mark of "different." The mainstream is now biodynamic. Pollution and soil contamination remain a growing problem, mainly from cars in the now crowded town. Water management is in the hands of the weather gods. But all in all, good teas are getting better even as the ones destined for low end iced tea and bags slide towards mediocrity.

The strategic agenda for success in producing fine tea and making an operating profit (Sri Lanka's average export price is $3 a kilo and production costs $3.50.) is:

Restore soil fertility levels through manure, mulch, straw, grading.

Obtain new clonal cultivars through research labs, government services that meet specific needs (e.g., water, nitrogen use).

Set up nurseries for clonal bushes to develop (1-4 years); replenish fields with a mix of plants to ensure genetic variety (vital given the nature of tea bush seed production).

Restore soil depth. Take depleted land out of production and add natural composting and terracing.

Implement eco-friendly management, not elimination, of widely and wildly prevalent pests, through natural pesticides, shade-trees and mixing in of flowers and shrubs.

Manage the bushes through 1-2 year pruning, spacing, infilling cycle.

Implement appropriate technology: production, logistics, monitoring.

Explore the mountains first

It's neither surprising nor complicated that great tea comes from great terroir, great management and great methods. It's not so obvious where to find these at a price you are comfortable with. The suggestions here don't lock you in and are certainly not based on snobbery. They just help guide you in expanding your exploration of teas that you haven't come across.

There are too many teas for anyone to sample in a lifetime. Just a few years ago, the practical choice space was very narrow: a limited range of specialty stores outside shopping centers, mainly for the affluent. There were few online providers. Premium teas meant ultra-premium prices.

None of this applies today. Now that Amazon lists over 100,000 teas, this is a new game. Online sellers have expanded the breadth and depth of the market: the range of teas and the varieties within the categories. Oolongs are only 2% of the US fine teas market, but Amazon alone offers over a thousand, including some outstanding Alishan High Mountain, milk and kingshuan oolongs.

There are 17,000 black teas listed on Amazon, which announced in mid-2016 that it will market its own private brands, under the Happy Belly label. (Happy Belly Lady Grey Green?) You can find very good teas easily. You can also be caught unawares (or uninformed) by a mass of mediocre ones; well over 16 of the 17 thousand can't be above average, by definition. The main question, given a wider and wider range of choices, is where to start?

Pick your mountain.

Making Tea: from Bush to Cup

The chemistry of the leaf

The simplest way to understand what produces so many differences among teas from the same green shoots on the same bush is through a short science tutorial: *The Tea Leaf as Chemistry Lab*.

On the bush, the leaf looks like just about any foliage and the tea that goes into your pot or cup is a heap of apparently inert, dry, brittle pieces of varying sizes, from a few centimeters for whole leaf down to sub-millimeter dust in a tea bag.

Inside, the leaf is anything but inert. It is immensely dynamic in its interactions with oxygen, heat, moisture and pressure. The rich complexity of flavors and variety of aromas and aftertastes emerge from the traces of over six *hundred* active "odorous compounds" that are diffused or dissipated through heating, drying, rolling, and in some instances infusion of flower petals.

The Artisan tradition of tea making is rather like alchemy. It is science in practice, evolved through long experiments and learning. The medieval alchemists are often seen as frauds or buffoons trying to turn lead into gold. In fact, many were brilliant technicians who found out what worked even with no theoretical base to draw on.

The tea masters (gender roles have been very, very marked in this ancient industry, together with caste and tribal boundaries) have similarly evolved a meticulous expertise. This is exquisitely fine-tuned to every detail of context, conditions, timing, and even individual patches of plants.

You're paying for the alchemist in buying Artisan teas. But there's a growing body of research that is bringing out the scientific grounding and principles underlying the tea makers' intuitions. The science is emerging via such tools as gas chromatography, spectrometry and molecular analysis. It confirms that the skilled crafters of tea have got it right.

The basic choice that a tea producer makes is how much to allow the harvested leaf to interact with the air and heat. Green teas minimize this oxidation, quickly steaming or pan-frying the leaf to control it, while black teas are fully oxidated through withering and rolling that releases a flow of enzymes. Oolongs range from near green 10% oxidation up to near black 80%. The key alchemic decision is timing the "kill the green" halting of oxidation, also termed de-enzyming and fixing.

| Tie Guan Yi 40% oxidation | Bao Zhong 10% | Da Hong Pao 80% |
| Iron Goddess of Mercy | Pouchong | Big Red Robe |

Three classic oolongs, all with wide range of grades, from excellent everyday to ultraluxury. Oolongs are always aromatic. Taiwan is matching and even exceeding China's best.

The choice of degree of oxidation obviously is based on instincts and experience in manipulating the leaf's chemistry. It is leveraged by expert on the spot judgment in the exact details and timing that make every production batch different enough to be identified in labeling and marketing. None of the distinctive pellet, ball, tight, loose, coiled, long, compressed shapes of oolongs are either an accident or ornamental.

In many instances, they are formed to unfold in the cup to create the equivalent of time-release capsules, with a single spoonful of dry leaf expanding to half a cup of steeped tea as shown in the middle image below.

The oolong craft: High mountain smallholdings; highly individualized "fixing" oxidation; shaping, curling, twisting the leaf; modulated variety and complexity

On the left is a picture of bushes being plucked in Taiwan, which now makes some of the finest oolongs anywhere. It started a millennium or so after the Chinese but has aggressively added plenty of modern science to the ancient craft.

The third image shows three oolongs that could have come from the very same bushes as those in the first one but look as if they are entirely different in leaf and liquor. Just minor variances in timing, heat and rolling change the chemical structure of the tea. In general, oolongs are crafted to open and expand when brewed: the middle image shows a single teaspoon of an Iron Goddess oolong unfolding to fill almost half the cup.

Keep in mind that the processing methods and use of CTC and other machines break the leaf up to lose much of its compound-making. It's a little like flash-freezing vegetables. They will be less complex than fresh unprocessed ones. They lurk on the bottom of the cup, not float.

Along with the hundreds of main compounds, there are thousands of others in a single leaf, along with over thirty mineral trace elements. A few are near unique to tea. Theanine, for example, gives it part of its umami savory and frothy flavor (it's a Japanese term.) It is found elsewhere in natural form only in a rare mushroom and herbal root.

Theanine illustrates this combination of chemistry lab and alchemist craft. It was first exploited to make gyokuro, the Japanese green tea that is one of the highest rated in the world. Gyokuro has been produced in Uji Province in Japan since 1835. A few farmers were covering their bushes with straw to protect against frost. An enterprising merchant noted that the teas had an unusual stickiness that gave them a uniquely sweet and full flavor. Now, the scientific base is well understood, but it was not until 1948 that theanine was recognized and extracted.

The straw covers that coddle the bushes are replaced by blankets for the last week or so before harvesting. This reduces photosynthesis and locks in the chlorophyll to add a dark green, low-tannin and hence slightly sweet character. The full name for theanine is L-γ-glutamylethylamide and N^5-ethyl-L-glutamine and it is an amino acid analogue of the proteinogenic amino acids L-glutamate and L-glutamine. Of course, you don't need to add this to your vocabulary, but it serves to point out just how dynamic and subtle the chemistry of the lab is.

Gyokuro: darkest green of any tea, produced naturally by shading the bushes from the sun

What the leaf is made of

Three quarters of the plucked leaf is just moisture and one of the first steps in processing it is to gently reduce that through withering. This process is sensitive to sun, time, temperature and humidity. It is not just a matter of drying out the leaf but activating the lab.

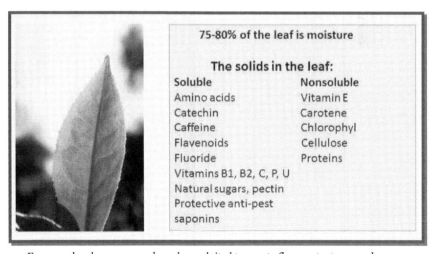

75-80% of the leaf is moisture

The solids in the leaf:

Soluble	Nonsoluble
Amino acids	Vitamin E
Catechin	Carotene
Caffeine	Chlorophyl
Flavenoids	Cellulose
Fluoride	Proteins
Vitamins B1, B2, C, P, U	
Natural sugars, pectin	
Protective anti-pest saponins	

Every molecular compound can be exploited to create flavors, textures and aromas

There are a few of these terms that are worth adding to your vocabulary because they are useful in descriptions of teas, reviews and identification of important aspects of varieties.

These are the main ones with a summary of their relevance to your own tea choices:

Oxidation	The critical stage in processing the leaf that establishes the degree and speed of its interaction with oxygen. Think of it as air-cooking; like sautéing or basting, it's subtle, precise and far more than just ripening and drying. Determines tea color: Black: fully oxidated, Oolongs: 10-80%, Green, low oxidation, White: none
Antioxidants	Molecular structures that inhibit the spread of "free radical" cells that damage the body's' stable chemistry; examples Vitamin A, C, E, betacarotenes. Synthetic and natural
Polyphenols	Natural antioxidant plant compounds largely found in fruits and vegetables; 8,000 known
Flavonoids	A broad category of polyphenols: water-soluble and biologically active pigments and other sources of nutrient that give tea – and fruits – their distinctive colors, tastes and aromas (6,000)
Flavonols	Subgroups of flavonoids, with distinctive potential health benefits: Quercetins, kaempferts, catechins, (4,000)
Catechins	The most studied and medically promising antioxidant, high levels in green tea; variants E, CG, etc. EGCG:epi-gallo-catechin-gallate
Tannins	Natural compounds prevalent in skins of grapes, bananas. Provide color and add to astringent taste. theaflavins. thearubigins
Caffeine	Mild psychoactive drug, safe in small doses, stimulant. Generated by the tea leaf as natural pesticide

It's the soluble compounds that make tea interesting in its science and practical dynamics. These build up, are released, combine, dissolve and interact in stages. Some, for instance, become activated in the very first step in processing, the withering. Others are brought out in the rolling that breaks up the cellular structure of the leaf.

Many are sensitive to a few degrees of change in external temperature, daily shifts in moisture on the bushes, or a half minute of added brewing time. The craft by which the chemical reactions are balanced and optimized requires a skilled overseer. It's highly situational and adaptive. And to some degree opportunistic. Economic forces and climate changing are leading many producers to corner-cut.

Oxidation: Determining color and basic taste

Oxidation involves no additives. It breaks down a stable structure, with oxygen always playing a part. When you cut an apple, it starts to turn brown. Oxygen and water rust iron. Breaking up a tea bush leaf stimulates the reactions of its many enzymes with oxygen. This activates compounds that give the different types of tea their flavors and their medicinal properties.

Plus their color. The catechin compounds in the leaf are converted into theaflavins and thearubigins. Theaflavins give tea its bright taste and briskness plus its yellow color. Thearubigins build body and fullness and create the orange to brown hues.

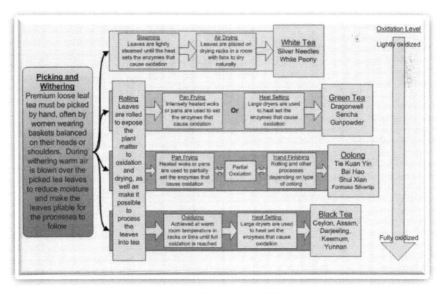

How teas get their color and flavors

There's no reason to learn about the intricate details of processing. That said, there are some general points worth considering. The first is, does it really matter? The answer to that is "Yes. Big time." The variations that make one Darjeeling, say, stand out as special versus another that is not quite as appealing come from distinctive skills and meticulous customization of leaf and method. The same applies to what makes white teas so exquisite and savory and oolongs so multi-dimensional in their body and balance of tastes and aromas.

From bush to cup: the logistics of tea

Many tea factories "buy in" their leaf from local growers. Some Artisan regions work as cooperatives in processing their leaf. Large farms, not surprisingly, operate large factories that are more and more automated. The tea you purchase doesn't magically appear on the shelf. How it gets there has a substantial impact on its quality, especially freshness, and on what it ends up being formally described as: a mutt or a pedigree, an anonymous "blend of teas" or a showpiece name.

From both a business and a shopper perspective, there are three main sets of links in the tea supply chain: (1) *Production*: growing and making the tea, (2) *Logistics*: managing procurement, certification, shipping and packaging, and (3) *Distribution*: marketing, branding and selling it. Consciously or not, regular tea drinkers focus on one of these and evolve their heuristics: rules of thumb for quickly assessing brands or tea types to look out for or avoid, how to spot a good deal, or indicators of quality.

Each of the three stages is a set of demanding processes, such as harvesting and rolling (production), auctioning and import inspection (logistics), and pricing and shelf placement (distribution). Each points to a primary focus for heuristics: either Which? How? or Who? For Production, it's *which* tea and for Distribution, *who* to buy from.

The catch is that it is easy to throw light on the Growing and Distribution stages – the tea itself and how it is marketed and sold – but the middle Logistics link is cloud-covered. It's all about the question "*How*?" and the difference that the answer makes: *How* does the tea get from the factory where it is processed to you?

The answer encompasses all the supply chain steps in moving the tea through storage, auctions, local trucking, direct sale contracts, export shipping, inspection, packaging, blending, customs, wholesaling, and so on.

The logistics of tea have always been inefficient, fragmented and cumbersome. Gardens may be scattered across remote mountainous regions. Production is highly seasonal. Transportation, storage and shipping vary widely in quality, security and reliability.

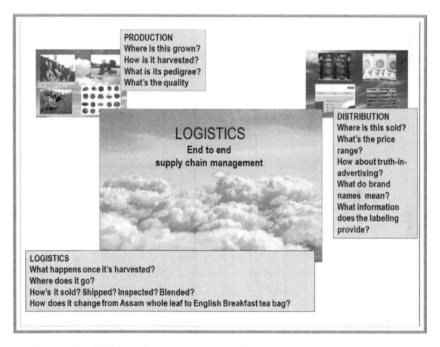

"Quality" and "value" depend on end-to-end excellence in growing and processing the tea,
fast, reliable coordination to feed it into the selling outlets.

Here's a slightly stereotyped summary of bush-cup supply chains:
Bulk logistics has been the strength of the major brands: contracting for leaf from large producers or the firm's own farms, cargo shipment to blending, packaging and distribution centers.

Cash-and-Carry logistics is at the other extreme. It has

historically sourced supplies on an as-needed basis via auctions, brokers and wholesalers and used agents for shipping to obtain economies of scale. It sells to packagers and blenders who make and distribute the final products.

Direct logistics fills the gap between the systemic integrated bulk and more ad hoc cash-and-carry extremes, focusing on improvement in inventory management and custom shipping. The goal is to be able to scale to gain the efficiency and cost advantages of bulk logistics, while maintaining the flexibility and responsiveness of cash-and-carry.

For you as a tea buyer, the two indicators of value are inventory and freshness. (1) What is the range of teas the firm offers and how competitively they are priced and (2) How fresh the tea is in packaging and fast delivery.

The gap between best and typical practice today is wide and a major factor to consider in shopping. Here's a broad summary, with implications for your choices summarized in the left-hand column.

	Best practice	Typical standard
	2-8 weeks bush to buyer Largely small batch	24 weeks or more High vertical integration
Freshness Same tea, same source may be 10 times fresher than one that seems identical	Direct grower/seller relationships Protected storage, vacuum-packing	Many intermediaries Weak inventory quality control
Origin The identification of the tea as special may hide a mediocre mix	Precise estate, region, quality name, grade Clear grower information	Re-exporting, country of origin loopholes Limited information on quality, sourcing
Packaging Legally, only ingredients list factual: what it doesn't include is often key	Certified ingredients, quality, testing Truth in advertising, disclosure	Marketing hype, few legal restrictions Private blends, bulk sales Counterfeits, adulteration
Shipping Sea container: $1 per kg Small shipment: (under 25 kg) $20 per kg	Tight inspection, testing, regulatory compliance Small package international services	Sea cargo transportation. Bulk handling, disguised intermediaries Export restrictions

How do you know how fresh your tea will be?

Freshness is the first test of what's happening behind the cloud cover. Say you are looking at three Darjeelings from the same estate and harvest but a different seller. Before you pick among them, how can you tell which will be more fresh when you get it?

Does that matter? Oh, yes! Does it vary much? Yes, yes and yes – oh, and add "!!!!") The rule of thumb here is that tea begins to deteriorate and lose its special flavors and aromas within six weeks and should preferably be consumed within six months of its being harvested. It will stay fresh if it is vacuum packed quickly after processing and then stored in climate-controlled warehousing.

Packaging is key for shipping, too: international air freight versus local transport from factories, multiple intermediaries in auctioning, brokering and wholesaling, traditional bagging for sea shipping (which often involves delays of a month or so at the port) and "hydroscopic" absorption of moisture, fumes and even chemicals along the many steps in local storage and transportation.

The time for Darjeelings to reach you ranges from two weeks or less (best practice logistics) to around six months (standard practice). The average time for a harvested China green tea to reach the US buyer is one *year*. When you pay a premium for a superb pre-Chingming spring tea that is harvested on the exact right *week* of the year, it's the How it gets to you, not the Which tea it is or Who sells it that matters most. As for Japanese senchas, here's a rule of thumb: unless the seller receives the tea from an elite small farmer and sends it to you by expedited delivery, try a China oolong instead.

The most complicated aspect of Logistics that is deliberately kept cloudy is just what a tea is and where it comes from. Here are a few quick examples that are likely to surprise you.

"Gathered from the prestigious highlands of Sri Lanka's Uwa region", may well contain 20-40% cheap imported machine-processed tea from Africa. The rules on "country of origin" and re-exporting distinguish between growing, packaging and blending a tea.

So, it is not difficult to make a tea appear to be from a prestigious source. You won't see Argentina listed as where most US green tea imports come from. There's a legal difference between just blending and packaging teas and doing something with them that is "value-adding." Vietnamese and Thai tea bulk shipped to Keelung Harbor may be re-exported as Taiwanese. Neither by itself can command a Taiwan price premium, which doubles profits but lowers quality.

Many of the teas you see in a specialty store are the same as those in any health food chain or grocery that has a tea section. Owners buy from wholesalers because they cannot afford the very high unit shipping costs of imports nor have the resources to maintain multiple relationships. They will generally have a few good pedigree teas that are sourced from a grower since these draw customers and provide higher prices. But, alas, in general their teas are ordinary and generic.

These examples are the tip of a giant iceberg and there is no way you can or should want to understand the bewildering details of the global tea supply chain. Here are some simple guides and screenings:

Look for a supplier that is close to the growers in relationships and geography, with direct and fast service links to you, the buyer. That will shift you to buying direct from growers and online tea specialists.

Avoid the mall palaces. The high-end tea retailers and gourmet stores sell ambience and marketing gloss. Their teas are weak practice in terms of Logistics and prices generally double what you should be paying. One major problem they face is that stocking 50-150 national stores with fresh, seasonal and low volume Artisan tea just can't be done without compromises.

Don't buy blends in tins where the main marketing is prestige, design and fancy sounding name. The tin is cheap to source and looks attractive but the tea will be a mass market, standardized purchase from a packager. Prices for Christmas time teas can be absurd.

Don't expect too much from the specialty store. Enjoy the atmosphere, try out samples and chat with a knowledgeable enthusiast owner. This is the bookstore/Amazon transformation once again. Specialty stores can't match the new online supply chain wizards so must create something special in the shopping experience.

Read the ingredients. The ingredient list is legally regulated but the marketing fluff and puff is not. So, the package says "Hand-plucked from mountain bushes in China's Yunnan Province." The ingredients say "product of multiple countries," "green tea." Go with the ingredient list.

With many nationally distributed teas, there is often a signal of the compromise between quality of the product and of logistics. Wherever you see mention of "Packaged for us in" or "Manufactured in" think factory and warehouse not mountain slopes and Artisans at work.

Here is the guide to what the labels tell you by what they *don't* state:

Ingredient list says	Really means
Imported black tea	Lower grades of no fixed abode or pedigree; blended from as many as 30 countries
Green tea, black tea	Cheap, low grade machine-processed, non-whole leaf
A blend of fine teas	Bulk stuff, probably supplied by contract packager, blender
A blend of X, Y and Z (e.g., Assam, Ceylon, Kenya)	A little of the good stuff and lots of filler
An exotic blend of	Overpriced

A short note on tea grades: forget orange pekoe

By far the most frustrating aspect of assessing tea quality is the lack of common grading systems that carry legal and industry weight. There's nothing to match the French appellation controlée framework for wines or the USDA Prime/Choice meat classifications.

The *Tea Tips* recommendation is basically to ignore all the ratings and leave them to specialists. There are a few rules of thumb to apply but, all in all, even an experienced tea lover will find it difficult to make sense of the often-arbitrary classifications.

The most formalized system is that used in the Indian tea industry, where auctions have been long the dominant supply chain base. (They are moving online and eliminating the power and often game-playing of key players in the market oligopolies.) This is the Pekoe classification. A variant is used in Ceylon. It provided bidders with basic information they needed.

China and Japan have systems that vary in their formalization and rate quality, whereas the pekoe classifications essentially relate to appearance, which is correlated with but not equivalent to it. Taiwan is the most rigorous in efforts to set government-defined and monitored standards for grading quality. It is the only system that rates flavor. The scoring that is a formal competition is 20% appearance, 20% aroma and 60% flavor. A Gold Medal oolong is a standout, in proven quality plus of course in price.

When you see that a tea is an "Orange Pekoe" (OP) black, the image that forms in your mind is most probably that this is a special tea. In fact, orange pekoe is not a tea but one of over 30 essentially judgmental assessments of the wholeness and condition of the tea leaf that is packaged and sold to tea drinkers. Above OP is a syllable load of tippy, golden, flowery and fine gradations. Below it is broken leaf, fannings and dust. So, basically all Orange Pekoe means is average and OK.

As with, say, strawberries, a high grade "flowery" and "tippy" tea that includes just the few most tender leaves is more likely to make for the equivalent of a good dessert than broken up shreds that correspond to hard, unripe and deformed berries. But wild strawberries taste wonderful even if they don't look perfect and include a few throwaways. There are some teas where the broken leaf is still good. Some, but not many.

The Dutch, who preceded even the British in the colonial tea trade, created the term "orange pekoe." Orange refers to the ruling House of Orange and appears to have emerged as an indicator of a Royal warrant. Pekoe is probably a corruption of Bai Hoa, the white tips on a bud that signal superior appearance.

The collage below summarizes the grading and lists the characteristics of the top whole leaf ones. There are similar divisions within the lower categories. Next to the description of each category is an image of the leaf. On the right is a standard picture of where on the bush the leaves in the top grades come from. Ceylon uses a related system, with "tippy" and "flowery" standing for good leaf and "dust" for just that. OP is just an anchor point: average for a whole leaf tea.

Distinguishing between, say, an FTFGOP – Special Finest Tippy Golden Flowery Orange Pekoe ("Still Far Too Good For Ordinary People") – and another high grade TGFOP requires training, experience and expertise, but tea shoppers can easily see the difference between the whole leaf at the top and the other three pictures. However, since they rarely open an unused tea bag to see what it contains, it may come as a surprise that that a "Finest organic Ceylon black tea" is made up of shakings that are the size equivalent of salt.

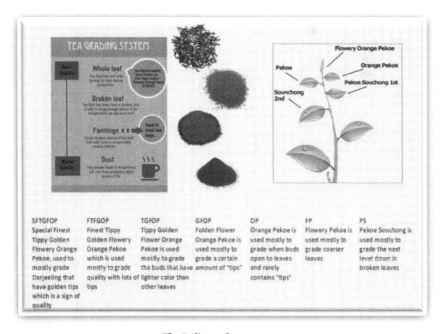

The Indian pekoe system

The Ceylon pekoe system is a little bewildering and does not correspond to the Indian one. Orange pekoe is the highest grade, Broken OP the most sought after, and Broken OP Fanning the most common.

Teas to try and why

A "portfolio" of teas

Tea preferences are highly individualized and there are no "bests"; best for you is a function of taste, flavor, price, convenience, sweetness, fullness, lightness, healthiness, brand, experience, curiosity and, well, just about anything.

The aim of *Tea Tips* is to help you find your own way around the wide world of tea. But it seems useful to offer some suggestions that provide an orientation for your exploration, with the strong caveat that they are just that: suggestions. They cover the main groupings and highlight teas that are some of, but not the only, outstanding choices within them.

Here's the summary mapping:

Category	Regions that stand out	Specific teas to try
Essential black teas	Assams: The lowland biggest region Darjeeling : The peak of tea	Harmutty, Mangalam, Halmari Castleton, Goomtee, Puttabong, Margaret's Hope, Thurbo, Clonal AV2
Black teas that add a difference	Ceylons: Variety and style Nepal: Good, getting better Nilgiri: Plain and resurgent China congou	Kenilworth, New Vithanakande, Lumbin, Court Lodge, Lover's Leap Guranse, Ilam, Kanyam Glendale, Craigmore, Havukal Keemun Panda, Mao Feng, Yunnan tips and Dian Hong
Smooth greens, whites	China: Nothing bitter Japan: Green themes Whites: Light, bright, filling	Pi Lo Chun, Mao Feng, Jasmine Pearls Sencha, Kukicha, Houjicha Silver Needle, White Peony, Shou Mei
Complex crafted teas	Oolongs: Art of tea masters Puehrs: Bricks, bings, bowls,	Tie Guan Yin; Taiwan Alishan, Wuyi Dan Cong

These are just one tea drinker's selection of a broad portfolio of teas to try that are likely to turn up a few grabbers, pleasant surprises and soon to be staples in your tea stash. But they are just fifty or so out of thousands of choices. They are all good, though, and unless otherwise stated, the prices are in the $4-6 an ounce price range: 30 to 50 cents a cup. The logic in presenting them is that before you can say "I know what I like", you must know what there is out there for you to like:

> *Essential black teas*: Selections from the two dominant regions for the premium teas that are most widely grown and sold: Assam and Darjeeling.
>
> *Black tea extras*: Teas that stand out as "different" from the essentials and may fit just what you personally like: Ceylon, China congou, Nilgiri and Nepal.
>
> *Smooth greens and whites*: Lighter teas where you may have avoided or disliked the generic ones but that offer you something special once you explore the styles and types: selected China greens, Japanese teas and white teas.
>
> *Complex crafted teas*: Ones that you need more knowledge and guidance to be comfortable in finding and choosing from among their specialized and distinctive characteristics: China puehrs and the oolongs of China and Taiwan.

The concept of a "portfolio" is that you mix and match to balance your cupboardful. The main criteria in picking the highlighted teas are that they be interesting, good value and appealin to most palates. Nothing too subtle or bland or a little weird.

Alas, "weird" precludes Lapsong Souchongs that warm your heart and curl your toes or the old-aged puehrs that can make you feel you are in the middle of a farm with the new-tilled soil broadcasting its aromas after a rain shower – wonderful, but that's for you to discover unadvised and unnudged. (Puehr is surely the only beverage where an enthusiastic reviewer serenades one for its "distinctive character of dirt and mud, along with a faint but clear rotting-fish note.")

There are regions left off the portfolio of suggestions. They offer a few standouts in otherwise commodity bulk Agribusiness produce. African teas, for instance, are 90% machine-harvested CTC tea bag fodder, but Kenya's Milima is a pleasing and mellow Orthodox tea. Several of Indonesia's Malabar estate blacks are outstanding.

There are also interesting teas hidden across the globe that are more and more becoming visible via the spotlight of the Web. If you want to do a tea snob one-upmanship riff, offer your guests the unusual and excellent Nui Giang, Yen Bai wild boar Vietnamese black. It's named for the hills where tribe folk roam to locate the leaf they pick from trees aged 200-800 years (in ad-speak measurements, anyway) that they bring in to the village factory.

Or you can pull out the Russian Black Sea Krasnodar Solohaul estate Alpine black, unusual in that there are no insects targeting the unusual. The leaves mature longer and build a chocolatey tea that is very highly praised in reviews.

Both teas are a reminder that even after three or more thousand years and even in the age of over a trillion cups consumed globally each year, fine tea is basically built around the opposite of advantages of scale: a small locale, with eccentric climate and hills, a dedicated artisan smallholder community, and batch/seasonal production of an unusual tea.

Teas like these are worth keeping a look out for, mainly through trusted online suppliers

What makes these two teas interesting options are their non-standardization; they are not typical of anything. The Yen Bai stands out as a source of the old tea trees that were the foundation of the Yunnan tea tradition but that are disappearing fast. It's unusual to make strong black whole leaf teas from this stock; Yen Bai is closer to

Assams than congous.

The Krasnodar comes from Sochi, where the Russian Winter Olympics were held in 2014. An entrepreneur set up a tea farm there in 1901; it's an isolated enclave that has evolved its own niche. The distinctive feature of the teas is that the leaf is not affected by insects. You can probably guess why, from the reference to the Olympics and the photo above; there just aren't any insect hordes and the bush has evolved to be hardy and weather-resistant.

These are off-beat teas, and not ones you are likely to look for. In non-snob mode, it's simpler to offer guests a Nilgiri or Keemun Panda instead. It is likely to be just as unfamiliar, costs less, and tastes great. That said, the Yen Bai and Krasnador are illustrative of the variety of teas increasingly accessible via online providers.

Please view the three sections as chats, not lectures, and "how about?" not "you should." The headings signal the goals – to help you find teas that will meet all your needs, preferences and pleasures.

Essential black teas: Assam, Darjeeling

Assam: the lowland biggest and often the best

If your core taste preference is for strong black teas, Assam is a good starting point for exploration. It is the largest single tea producing region in the world and the core of the British tea-drinking culture, which was never noted for subtlety or delicacy of flavor; Assams are best summarized as big.

The region now mainly produces CTC tea for blends in such full black teas as English Breakfast. These are grown on lowland farms, with harvesting throughout the year. The priority for Assam is productivity at the risk of loss of quality. It must increase its revenues in a market of declining prices. Exports have dropped by 12% in the last five years. Average quality has eroded.

There remain, though, some outstanding estates. In addition, there are many BOP grades – broken orange pekoe – that represent good value if you enjoy bold, wake-up, hearty, tart and bracing teas. These are all adjectives that come up again and again in ads and reviews. Here is the spectrum of Assam choices, with *very* approximate prices to show relative differences:

Assams are all big in flavor: the best are smoothly so and the poorer ones bitter.

The estate teas add their hint of sweetness to the base malty flavor of Assams. *Hamrutty* is an example of a black that is not bitter but very smooth. It is a warm coppery-brown in the cup and the leaf is flecked with gold tips; these tips are a common feature of great Assams and help soften the astringency common to most.

Halmari offers a wide range of both high end and broken leaf teas. *Mangalam*'s teas are lighter than most Assams, without losing their punch and robustness. It is investing heavily in clonal teas, ones developed in research to bring out specific nuances of flavor and to strengthen such characteristics as water use, root strength and resistance to pests. These are terrific buys.

Over half of India's tea comes from Assam. The best is superb. The average is good. The caveat is that low end quality is falling fast and many farms are failing. Social unrest is at crisis levels in many areas, with escalating poverty and violence. Wages are often unpaid for months. In a notorious incident in 2015, rioting workers burnt alive the owner of a plantation and his wife.

Climate change is already bringing shifts in the seasonal rains. The past three years have seen recurrent major floods. Government food subsidy cuts have been reduced further marginalizing tea worker families where the average daily wage is under $2.

Assam's history centers around its broad river, Brahmaputra, its tribal diversity and tea

This collage is impressionistic only; it's impossible to offer a simple, one-dimensional view of Assam tea, industry, society or politics. The images include, in the first row, the women workers who comprise 70% of the labor force, bringing their baskets of leaf to be weighed, and one a too typical victim of the massive flooding of the 2015-2016 period.

The second row shows a very poisonous snake coaxed from the tea bushes. Note the elephants in the bottom images heffalumping (to poach a lovely word from Winnie the Pooh) through the gardens. Assam's sprawling river, jungle and reserves are a wealth of diversity.

Tucked into the middle row, next to samples of the rich and bright colors of the tea that has made Assam so special, is the home of a family of tea workers. It's not fully representative; historically, Indian plantations have provided free housing, medical care and schooling to their "labor lines" but that is breaking down rapidly. Below the picture is a related news photo: army troops at a scene of civil protest against tea worker conditions.

The final picture is pivotal for the nature, quality and economics of tea, not just in Assam: the arrival of tea-plucking machines. Kenya and Sri Lanka are competing aggressively on the basis of both price and quality. Vietnam's low labor costs are cutting into CTC low grade markets. African teas have displaced Assam's previous dominance.

The *Tea Tips* recommendation about Assam teas is hesitant and iffy. The "if" is your liking for big teas and a recognition that there are plenty of bargains on the market. It comes with a "but" – but make sure you are shopping, whether online of in a store, somewhere where you will get quality, not just low price.

Darjeeling: The peak of tea

Darjeeling is a peak of tea in two senses. It is grown on the slopes of the third highest mountain in the world, Kangchmenjunga, standing out in the physical landscape of the Himalayas. Around ninety estates compete on reputation and identity for their black teas and expanding their efforts to become elite producers of whites, greens and oolongs.

All this can be a little far off in the clouds for many tea drinkers. Ninety estates, three main harvests, many seasonal patterns, different elevations, individual styles of production, and specialized selectivity in farming, harvesting and processing...

Overall, Darjeeling teas are not part of the daily scene that most tea drinkers either know about, come across or are alerted to. They often assume that Darjeeling is a single tea, rather than some hundreds of them. Fitting with its name recognition, captured in the cliché about it being the champagne of tea, Darjeeling is then seen as a "different" and "expensive" treat rather than an everyday pleasure – people don't drink champagne for breakfast daily.

High tea. Interesting weather patterns. Not an easy commute

Once you know enough about Darjeeling teas to be comfortable in exploring the options, you are quite likely to love them. That's not a certainty, of course, and some experts feel the teas are overrated and overpriced and that sometimes a new harvest results in a boring yield. That said, they often add that when the rain comes at the right time in spring and the leaves on the bushes are nutrition-rich from a nurturing winter, Darjeeling teas are magical.

Somewhere out there are magical Darjeelings for you. There is literally no other tea like it. Efforts to reproduce, transplant, imitate or clone it have failed again and again. It's unique: the peak of tea. Its heritage is built on black teas but there are growing moves to produce green, oolong and white ones, with varying results. Many of the Moonlight white teas, from outstanding estates like Castleton and Margaret's Hope, are superb.

But a substantial problem with the better oolongs and fewer standout greens are that their price is too often far higher than comparable teas from other countries. Darjeeling's labor-intensive operations leave it with the highest cost base in the industry.

That is increasingly unsustainable. Stick with Darjeeling blacks. (And grab Taiwan oolongs.) They are expensive but they can command a premium price for their premium place in the global market.

Darjeeling is all tea. That's its asset and its burden.
It lived on its history and must move beyond it to protect its future

How to choose Darjeeling teas

There is no typical Darjeeling. The black teas are marked by variety of garden, harvest, elevation, bush variety, and processing. They range in price from as inexpensive as a gussied-up bag to as costly as a cognac. They have increasingly different leaf characteristics and resulting subtleties in flavor and aroma. Here's a simple orientation to finding the ones for you:

Don't think of Darjeeling as a single tea. Even within an individual estate there are many differences among its teas. Here, for instance, is a close up on four 2015 autumn harvest teas from one of the medium sized gardens. These are all the "same" tea: Estate XYZ Darjeeling. They are all different.

Some of this comes from choice of bush: chinary may be in a section next to a clonal patch. Elevation and exposure to sun, exact soil profile and maturity of the plant are factors to tweak.

Same garden, same year, same harvest. Different Artisan crafting.

Start your exploration by getting a sense of the distinctive style of the first flush (Spring harvest) and second flush (Summer). These are separated by just a few months but produce a difference analogous to the Burgundy versus Bordeaux distinction for red wines.

A Goomtee estate first flush may be your own choice, over a Castleton second flush, or you may prefer a Goomtee 2nd versus a Castleton 1st. The combination of estate and flush is at the base of Darjeeling variety. There are four flushes, with the monsoon and autumn ones of lesser fullness and zip. The first flush is often summarized as light and astringent and the second as full-bodied muscatel.

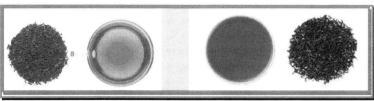

Goomtee first flush   *Castleton second flush*

Get a sense of the main "flags" that broadly indicate quality and value without your having to understand all the rich and complex Darjeeling tea lore: Estate, Grade, Harvest. There's enough information in just these three categories to give you a clear idea of the relative attractiveness of each of the teas for you.

Learn the marketing traps of "Darjeeling tea" and where to buy and what to avoid. One simple and firm rule for shopping for Darjeelings in a supermarket is: Don't. Buy a decent English Breakfast instead.

The stuff in a bag is regional plains CTC, or cheap broken leaf and fannings bought from growers' leftovers. The yield from lowland farming is 3,000 kilos per hectare. The Orthodox tea harvest is 500. The gap of 2,500, a factor of five, is not two leaves and a bud.

Expand your exploration selectively to include oolongs, greens and whites but focus first on black teas. Similarly, try estate teas and then consider good value blends. The *Tea Tip* subjective, opinion-only, start off recommendation for value, reliability and satisfying all-around flavor is Thurbo, Goomtee and Margaret's Hope.

Quality and pedigree flags

The range of Darjeeling flavors shows up most clearly in the variety of seasonal harvests.

Harvest	Season	Characteristics
First/Spring flush	After dormant winter, Feb-mid-April	Light, bright, just a little astringent; fragrant floral aromas

Second/Summer flush	May-June	Fuller flavor, treasured "muscatel" mellowness; complex richness of taste
Monsoon	July-Sept, rainy season	Stronger: not worth paying much for and generally just a mediocre base for a breakfast blend.
Autumn	Oct-Nov	Lighter, delicate; not as complex in flavors as 1st and 2nd flushes.

In many regions of the world teas are harvested year-round, as much as every few weeks, with rest periods. In some, the first Spring harvest is by far the best; pre-Chingming (the Spring festival) China greens are premium and prized. With Darjeelings there are two bests, the Spring first and Summer second flush and two later and lesser ones. If the flush is not mentioned, you will be getting a mix of harvests in a blend.

Focusing on the two main flushes is a better option than a blend, though there are some good ones on the market. Those will generally be a mix of leaf from several estates or from grades that are not quite in the top category, a little broken up and not as well-formed. For the beginner, blends may seem an obvious choice but they tend to be a little disappointing in that they average out the distinctive characteristics of each individual ingredient.

For black teas, only first (or "spring"), second ("summer") and autumn flushes are pedigree: monsoon and in-between ones mean "you can do better." Autumn flush teas are what one expert terms "muted" versions of second flush ones. They can be very good buys.

Don't bother with in-between and monsoon harvests. South Indian and Nepalese teas are strengthening the quality of their winter "frost" teas and there are some terrific Nilgiris and Nepals but try these after you map out your preferences and favorite estates.

The next flag is not as important as it once was and can be misleading. This is the grade of the finished leaf's wholeness and appearance. There are over thirty grades. SFTGFOP is the very highest. Almost every elite garden will be SFTx or FTx. If you start seeing a B in the grade, the quality is lower. It stands for Broken leaf. The shorter the grade, the more ordinary it is: FOP, BOP, GOP, etc. OP is a minor exception. It's average whole leaf that doesn't get an adjective added.

Focus on the broader categories that they reflect:

Whole leaf: Look for FTG. Don't worry about whether it has an S for special in front of it and ignore any number at the end SFTGFOP1 or Spl, another special claim. To some extent, the longer the acronym the superior the leaf's finish but all you really want is some indicator that this is premium, not special ultra-premium (reserve).

FOP and OP are so-so and generally well-priced. They reflect less than perfect processing results that loses a little of some element of flavor or aroma.

Broken leaf: Here, the loss is more marked and by and large this is not a good deal. Darjeeling prices are high and you can get a better quality whole leaf Ceylon or Assam for the same amount. FOP, maybe. BOP, not really,

Fannings: These are indicated by the F being at the end not the beginning: GFOF, FOF, for Golden and Flowery. If it's fannings, it doesn't matter if it's G, F or whatever, there's no formal definition beyond fragments that are bigger than dust. In practice, it's re-used rejects from processing that fall through the sieve in the final sifting.

Dust: Try some instant coffee instead.

This summary applies to Assam and all other Indian and Nepalese black teas, as well as Darjeeling. The main differences are that you will see many higher grade Assams that are TGF, below the top SFTGF and FTGF. Far more of the teas for sale will be Broken OP. The Agribusiness mainstream of CTC is also part of the scene; Darjeeling is strictly Orthodox processing, not rotorvane machined.

Sampling the garden estates

The first/second flush choice is the main step in selection of Darjeelings. Now comes the more arbitrary step: choose an estate. Think of that not as picking a tea but like selecting a restaurant. There are so many outstanding estates, with so many individual strengths and so much special expertise that it is impossible to recommend any one of the best above the other bests. Every Darjeeling lover has a personal list.

With deep hesitation, here are a few suggestions. They are just that. A search online of estates and offers from suppliers will give you a sense of the reputation and record of individual ones. You can't go wrong with Castleton, Goomtee, Puttabong, Margaret's Hope, Thurbo, Makaibari, Giddapahar, Ambootia, or Tindharia. Then there's Singtom, Rohini...

Just pick a few to try. Of the three "starters" suggested earlier, Margaret's Hope second flush is a joy and surprisingly inexpensive. Thurbo is reliable, with tippy teas at a good price. Goomtee is at the higher end in costs but has a wide range of distinctive teas.

The best way to get started is to buy sample packs online. The elite providers offer vacuum-packed 10 gram envelopes for $2-3, with many special deals. You can get, for instance, a collection of maybe ten first flush teas or even dozens of, say, breakfast Darjeelings at very attractive prices. 10 grams makes four cups of tea.

On a per unit basis, the samples cost about double what you'd pay per ounce from the same provider. But for $20 or less you can get a good sense of estates and their teas instead of risking the same amount on a hit or miss single purchase of a mid-range 100 grams (3.5 ounces). Make sure any sampler package mainly includes estate names and not generic blends, Earl Greys and flavored teas.

Buy online. There are a small number of excellent Indian providers, several fine US ones and the largest is German. The UK has some high end, but also high price, providers. Some of the gardens are marketing their teas direct to the customer. You can easily find every single Darjeeling tea on the market for sale online. Packaging has improved and shipping is fast and efficient.

Look for a supplier whose teas are presented by pedigree. Estate, Harvest, Leaf grade. You don't need fluff.

Black teas that add a difference

There are, of course, many black teas beyond the Indian heavy-lighter duo of Assam and Darjeeling. The four suggested in *Tea Tips* are (1) Sri Lanka, whose *Ceylon* teas include super individual regional blacks (and some truly outstanding white teas), (2) *Nilgiri*, an Indian tea that is a reliable and inexpensive choice, (3) *Nepal*, the rising complement and rival to Darjeeling, offering real bargains, and (4) *Chinese congou* black teas, often unfamiliar to tea drinkers who identify them with the British colonial producers and China with green teas.

Finally, and fulsomely, *Tea Tips* draws your attention to what is by far the most promising general development in the tea industry in general, with especial impact on Darjeelings: clonal teas.

Together, the six styles of tea reviewed here – these four plus Assam and Darjeeling – span a wide range of fullness and complexity. Here are the main relative characteristics:

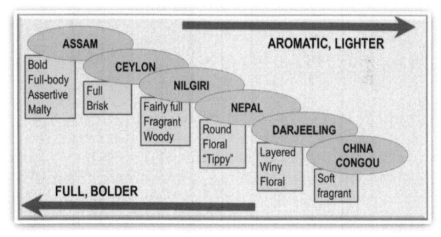

The outer pairs – Assam/Ceylon and Darjeeling/Congou – include many classic, pedigree teas. The less familiar middle Nilgiri/Nepal pair offers many bargains

Ceylon: variety and style

Sri Lanka is the third of the major players in the global industry, along with China and India. It is export-focused while their teas are mainly consumed domestically. It is about the size of West Virginia and is basically a set of tea farms.

The history and status of the Sri Lanka tea industry is complex and volatile, including near collapse after misguided nationalization and the impacts of twenty years of brutal civil war that ended only in the early 2000s. It expanded by competing with other major exporters of black teas suited for use in bags and blends.

It produces some very good teas; many experts rate it as the best overall maker of black teas and it offers several of the world's finest whites. The blacks are mostly full and brisk, in the Assam range but crisper. There's a pleasing variation among the regions, each with its microclimate and mountains. Kirksowold from Dimbula, for instance, is a full-bodied tea, though not particularly exciting, but then do you really want your tea to snarl at you at 7.30 a.m.? Nuwara Eliya Lover's Leap is much lighter. The best Ceylons share a brisk flavor and often fruity rather than floral aroma.

But, buyer beware. "Ceylon" or even "100% Ceylon" is not enough to merit your buying one. There are wide variations in quality and style between regions. The best quality Ceylon teas are grown at heights between 3,000 and 7,000 feet. The tea bushes "flush" weekly and are picked year-round. The best leaves come from higher elevations and are harvested in the drier seasons of February-March and August-September.

The *Tea Tips* recommendation is to start with a few teas to let your taste buds report back to you on whether this one is anchor tea status, one that sets your measure of "my" style of tea and a base for comparison with others: New Vithanakande from the lowlands of Ratnapura, Kenilworth from Kandy, and Nuwara Eliya's Court Lodge and Lover's Leap estates.

New Vithanakande Estate is a superb choice; it is full in strength and smooth, one of the best teas for routine drinking. The cost is very affordable. One online seller succinctly captures its distinctive character: the malty flavor of a Ceylon, the strength of an Assam, and the subtlety of a China black.

Kenilworth is in the same top league as the best Darjeeling estates. Its teas have a slightly liquorice flavor, and all in all are just what you'd expect a top rate black tea to be. There are fuller, more complex and aromatic Ceylons to pick from, but Kenilworth is a fine complement to them as well as to Darjeelings. Overall, it is one of the best value options on the market.

Along with these outstanding and well-priced options, get to know Ceylons by focusing on its top megamountain region, Nuwara Eliya. Its teas are complex and aromatic, a result of its combination of high elevation and cooler climate than the other main regions, which slows down the bush's growth. Court Lodge and Lover's Leap are two of the best estates.

Four truly outstanding teas from one of the world's greatest regions

The Sri Lanka Tea Board developed a certification program for 100% Ceylon Teas, which carry a Lion logo. This is a Geographic Indicator that trademarks the location rather than the tea.

Sri Lanka's government is highly active in marketing and quality control. Its very varied tea regions are a major part of its branding.

The Sri Lanka tea industry faces ongoing problems. Harvests have fallen for the past decade, due to weather and labor strikes. There is a shortage of skilled workers and heavy "politicizing" by the government, particularly in jobs being awarded based on connections and nepotism. Costs are higher than even India's and more than three times those of competitive Vietnamese producers that are aggressively targeting its main export markets. All this turmoil can make buying a Ceylon a matter of uncertainty and disappointment, but the best is reliable. The four suggestions are among the best.

Nilgiri: plain and resurgent

Nilgiri is well worth considering if you are looking for a medium-full, lower price black tea. It is lighter than Assams and Ceylons, and much less expensive than Darjeelings. There's nothing especially distinctive about it; one blogger summarized it as "cozy, pleasant, nice." But it's not bland, either. The best whole leaf is fragrant and full. It is lower in astringency than the Northern India teas. It's well worth seeking out.

Nilgiri is the second largest tea growing region of India, in the South East, at the opposite end of India from Assam and Darjeeling in the Himalayas. It thrived up to the 1990s by overproducing truly mediocre tea for the USSR market. When the Soviet buyers stopped coming as the economy crashed, so did Nilgiri.

Nilgiri teas are seeking an identity beyond the generic.

Now, the industry is being rebuilt. CTC is still the economic base as an ingredient in flavored teas and blends. But estates like Glendale are making superior black teas and improving their greens and whites.

All in all, Nilgiris are well worth trying as a candidate for your daily breakfast routine. They sell for as little as $30 or so a pound, 15 cents a cup. There are relatively few standout names, but Glendale, Craigmore and Havukal have a solid and wide product range. Reviews of all three gardens consistently express a slight surprise about how unexpectedly aromatic, smooth and mouth-filling these teas are. Their winter frost teas are getting very positive reviews. These are a late harvest made practical by the Southern climate.

The *Tea Tips* suggestion is to sample a Nilgiri from a name estate; see if you like the style. Try a winter frost tea, keeping an eye out for the bargains that these offer during the year. The Craigmore frost tea sold for $2.50 an ounce – 20 cents a cup – in early 2017. This would be a good buy at double that.

Nepal: good tea, and part of a great social change

Nepal is probably not on your list of teas to buy but they should be. Its best teas are good and getting better and better. A few names are emerging as an excellent balance of quality and price: Guranse, Ilam and Antu Valley and Kanyam.

Nepal's tea industry is rapidly reaching scale, with grants that enable purchases of low cost Japanese and Chinese machines, improved international distribution.

The major potential blockage to growth is almost sure to center around the three words that capture Nepalese politics: instability, incompetence and venality. Those are the more positive elements.

The tea industry has talent, terrain, access to international funding and expertise, and cost advantages and there is still reason for cautious optimism about its development. Guranse black tea in particular is very good indeed. It is not quite the same in taste as Darjeeling, though many experts claim that except for the very best and most expensive Darjeelings, Nepal is offering an equally attractive and less expensive complement that is typically slightly softer and a little woodier.

Guranse estate is the center of the development of the new Nepali tea industry and in the forefront of techniques. All the tea that it produces is organic. The bushes are grown from clones, not seeds. It is experimenting with varietals from young Darjeeling mother bushes that are robust, disease resistant and flavorful.

In the lowlands, where most of the production is cheap CTC, plants are ready for harvesting in 3-5 years, but the Guranse high hill ones take around seven years before they are mature enough for plucking. It was founded only in 1990 and was well-positioned to exploit new China clonal bushes on unspoiled terrain. It also buys in leaf of high quality from over seventy smallholder farms.

Until recently, Nepalese teas were made for domestic consumption. Up to the 1950s, there were no roads into the region. The logistics of tea transportation obviously impeded the growth of an export market, but ingenuity and money created a thriving smuggling business. Teas from Nepal were brought into the adjoining Indian territory and sold as Darjeeling or mixed into it.

Legitimate export was complex, with the teas being sent to Kolkata for auction by Indian brokers. Now, there are traders operating in Nepal who can ensure more visibility and better prices. But Nepal still lacks a strong reputation in the world market. The

Indian government imposed a 20% luxury tax on the import of foreign tea, which added to the cost of auctioning it through Kolkata.

As in China, the tea farms were government-owned and run by privileged insiders, often amateurs or well-connected ex-tea traders living off the guaranteed monopoly sales. When they were sold off to private owners in the 1990s, entrepreneurs realized that the industry was missing an opportunity. The Nepal Tree Crop Global Alliance and international agencies have invested substantial money to stimulate organic tea farming.

Guranse is the standout Nepalese tea, but others that are well worth trying include Kanyam factory, which makes pleasingly smooth and very slightly sweet inexpensive tea that is one of the bargains on today's market. It grows leaf at high altitude (6,000 feet). This gives it a concentrated flavor that comes from its being a slow growth tea. Antu Valley teas are light and inexpensive.

Kanyam Ilam: interesting vistas, traffic patterns, weather and farmland

Kanyam is a noted tourist attraction. Tea tourism is an expanding business across the mountain regions of China, India and Sri Lanka

Much Nepal tea, which includes a growing number of greens, is targeted to blends. The tightening of rules on labeling a tea as "Darjeeling" is stimulating the growth of "Himalayan" teas, especially in Germany, the largest global market for Darjeeling. They are worth sampling. In any case, Guranse is worth making a part of the black tea lover's stock.

Overall, Nepal teas are one of the great deals on the market. The greens are improving rapidly and are already a better buy than many Darjeeling ones. They will almost surely become even more competitive, for a variety of interrelated social, economic, technical and business factors. Essentially, Nepalese growers have more flexibility in investment and production, plus less dependence on fixed costs. It will be interesting to see how much of their future will involve the Artisan versus the Agribusiness path.

That's a question to ponder over a pot of Guranse black tea, definitely Artisan.

China congous: Keemun Panda

Black teas are mainly associated with the heritage of British colonialism: India, Ceylon, Kenya, Malaysia, Malawi and other African nations. That style has focused on strong, heavy teas that tend to be high on astringency. It's well worth trying a few China black teas, mostly known as congou, as a complement, contrast and lighter style.

These were very much a sideline and are still secondary in production and consumption to its greens and whites. 19th century demand in Europe expanded their cultivation. The Chinese refer to them as red teas. The intensity of black teas largely reflects how quickly they are oxidated. Assam teas are processed over a short period. China blacks are oxidated very slowly, making them softer. A simple test of the difference is that they don't have drinkers reaching out for milk or sugar.

Keemuns are the best and hold up well as a contrast and complement to Darjeelings, the standard-setter for blacks. They are more mellow than a Ceylon or Assam but still big and rich in flavor. They stand apart from the British colonial style as smokier and almost wine-like in taste.

Here's a China black basic menu: pick at random. The images are representative only; there are many variations in name and style. Key words are Keemun Panda and Mao Feng, Yunnan tips and Dian Hong. Medium grades of all these teas are excellent buys.

China black teas are a refined complement not alternative to Indian and Ceylon styles

The main characteristic of China black teas is their mellowness. That of the British colonial tradition is fullness. Qimen (Keemun) is the small town in Anhui noted for the "refined" methods its producers have evolved. These place an emphasis on preparing the leaf carefully before it is processed and oxidating it slowly, locking in its softer flavors. "Unrefined" tea making, by contrast, gets to work quickly on the fresh-plucked leaf to bring out its characteristics.

China black teas are a minor segment of the domestic market, where green teas dominate. While they have been produced for the standard thousand years or so routinely ascribed to just about anything in Chinese lore and legend, they mainly evolved to attract British traders. For a variety of economic and political reasons, China's tea exports virtually disappeared at end of the 19th century, left behind by the surge in Indian and Ceylon production. Congou became unfamiliar in the UK, US and other major markets. That's why they still remain overlooked by many tea lovers.

Keemuns deserve their reputation and you deserve to enjoy them. The best of all are Mao Feng, which means "hairpoint," for their fine hand-rolled leaves. Panda is the most widely known and a good starting point for exploring them. It is noted for its wiry, tight leaves that produce a rich liquor.

Panda is produced to last a long time and can be stored for years, maturing with age, becoming even mellower. The prices for Keemun Panda #1 are excellent for a tea which is so carefully made; they average 25 cents a cup, $50 a pound. Keemun Mao Feng is higher in price with more varieties; typically, it sells for close to 40 cents a cup. Both are excellent and you may find that they suit your palate better than the more familiar Indian style.

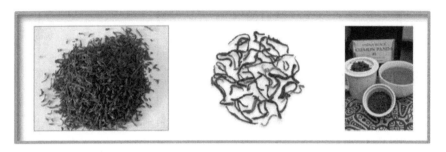

China Anhui province Keemun teas range widely, from basic organic black to hairpoint Mao Feng and Panda congou. All terrific: smooth, aromatic

Yunnan congous are a pleasing complement to Keemuns. They are noted for their golden tips and are robust but smooth. They are the least astringent of all blacks, provided they are not over-brewed. You will come across many with names like black tips, gold tips, and Dian Hong. Dian is Yunnan and hong red tea. They are often described as peppery.

The most common criticism is that Keemuns don't store well and can quickly lose their zippy taste. Many of the better English Breakfasts use Yunnan gold as a base. One supplier usefully summarizes Keemuns as the aristocrats of China blacks and Yunnans as their frugal cousin. Avoid the lower broken grades, which can be earthy and almost a puehr.

Going clonal: how about a nice cup of AV2?

Tea has largely lived on its history: the great regions, names and traditions. There's one area, though, where it's the future that looks glorious, rather than just the past. This is clonal teas from naturally evolved seedlings nursed through generations of complex and meticulous selection, nursing and propagation. The lead time from introduction to full scale production is typically at least seven years.

There are a few of these that are taking on an identity beyond the technical, rather like the distinction of grand cru and premier cru in French wines. One, AV2, stands out as, well, "magnifique!" Darjeeling tea lovers are recognizing it as adding a something extra to the already wide range of choices they have of pedigree black teas and increasingly outstanding whites, varied oolongs and improving greens. It's worth your looking directly for an AV2 clonal and then checking out the estate, description, reviews, prices.

Clonal teas change some element of the genetic structure of the bush and the molecular composition of the leaf. Successful varieties improve elements of crop yield, root strength, hardiness, resistance to blight, and water requirements. They have been widely adopted across the many tea growing countries in Asia and Africa, mainly for larger-scale production.

In Darjeeling, the focus has been on high end innovation, often by small scale operations. This may be summarized as the best estates making their best teas better. Here, the priority is on significantly transforming some aspect of quality in teas that already have an outstanding reputation. The result is a marked but subtle floral boost.

Three Darjeeling clonal cultivars, side by side: B157, P312, AV2

The clonals accentuate the tea flavors lightly and not harshly. They are not at all astringent. This makes the Moonlight whites from around ten estates match the reputation of even the superb Yunnan and Fujian Moonlights as among the very best teas on the market.

Each of the elite estates' AV2s offers some nuance of difference. They are often interblended with other clonals and established "chinary" and hybrid Sinensis/Assamica bushes. (Darjeeling clonals are named for the estate that created them: AV2 stands for Ambari

Vegetative.) Growing these teas is not mass farming but highly selective and meticulous crafting.

There are hundreds of clonal teas in China, Japan and East Africa. Development and deployment have been continuous for fifty years or so. AV2 may be the first that is a primary differentiator. That is, if instead of picking out an estate, first or second flush or grade (STGFOP), you search "Show me an AV2", would that ensure you an outstanding selection?

Simple answer: Yes.

Smooth greens and whites

Perhaps the most frequent comment that drinkers of standard teas, mostly bags of Earl Grey, English Breakfast and fruit/floral blends, make in conversations about new options is that they hate green tea. So they should, if that means the Agribusiness mass farmed anonymities.

It is difficult to make fine Artisan green teas. It is easy to make Agribusiness ones and it can be very profitable, especially if the marketers can ride the health bandwagon and imply that the green bag is intentionally meant to taste like plaster marinated in nail polish; that's what makes it so, so good for your health.

Green teas can taste so, so good and are probably a health aid, too. Here are the main factors that create the Artisan/Agribusiness green tea contrast.

	Artisan	Agribusiness
Terroir	Megamountains, biodiverse, seasonal climate, soil nutrients	Marginal lowland farms High pesticide, fertilizer needs
Leaf	Plucked; selected top buds, tender leaves	Sheared, no selection, lower, tougher leaf
Harvesting	Spring main; 2-3 through Autumn	Year round
Withering	Complex, critical: shaded open air, multiple methods, times, stirring, layering; tea master judgement on timing, steps	Standardized streamlining, heat-controlled rooms. Single pass, fast
Heating	Steaming, shaping semi- or fully-manually to tailor leaf compounds, chemistry	Baking/ highly automatable, fast
Batching	Each batch individual treatment, grading	None: standardized process flow, blending, bagging
Tea master	Chief chef; average age 50+; decision maker	Operations manager; production specialist
Time to market	3-6 months; 1 year storage life	Average 1 year; 1-2-year shelf life

Here's the punchline: there is no way a green tea that fits all the Agribusiness profile list can be other than grassy, vegetal and bitter.

It's fully reasonable to say "I hate green tea" when these are the choices. To find an "I love this" one, it's back to megamountain/region, pedigree name and the leaf.

The earlier description of Dragonwell production captures all this, including the selectivity of the harvesting in a few weeks after the spring pre-Chingming rains, the pan-frying where the workers' hands are bare to ensure they detect the exact heat and texture of the leaf, and the differences in grades that result from such factors as the smallholder's experience and reputation, location on Lion's Peak and even shading and scents from adjoining trees.

None of these applies to the green tea that gets bagged, used for iced and ready to drink teas, or made the base for health and diet supplements, extracts, and weight loss teas. The large tea farms that control export licenses have eroded quality in the interests of volume, with pesticides a growing concern. Money has been known to change hands to smooth regulatory inspection.

Green teas: never bitter, always subtle

Here's a selection of Artisan teas that are satisfying and smooth. There are hundreds of others that you may like more but these are all ones that are have some distinctive flavor that is full enough to stand out but isn't harsh or obtrusive.

China Jasmine Pearls: Superb. Perhaps *the* green tea for green tea haters. Infused with fresh jasmine petals, in tight balls that expand to release a subtly full flavor.

Japanese Sencha, Kukicha and Houjicha: Meet the taste preferences of most black tea drinkers. Uji sencha is a standout. Houjicha is smoothing and Kukicha adds a hint of smoky/woody dry taste. The three offer a gradation of sweetness/dryness and soothing/sharpness.

China Huangshan Mao Feng: Very, very slightly sweet and mild. Many grades. Perhaps the best of all the hundreds of China greens in terms of suiting the Western palate.

Pi Lo Chun: very light but full of complex flowery nuances.

Moroccan Mint: Fresh, piquant, stimulating. A pleasant

change. Very fresh balance between mint and China gunpowder green tea.

Jasmine pearl   Kukicha   Senchs   Mao Fneg   Moroocan mint   Pi Lo Chun

Six green teas that are different from standard tea bags as cheese is from chalk
(the comparison is close to literal)

China greens: Sweet and light

There are three obvious candidates for selecting an outstanding China green and then hundreds of others to explore. The ultra-elite are Dragonwell, Pi Lo Chun and Huangshan Mao Feng. They top just about every list of the ten best China teas. Dragonwell heads them. The *Tea Tips* suggestion is to leave this until you have calibrated if you like the China style and if so what you are looking for in terms of lightness, sweetness, fullness, etc.

China greens have evolved for thousands of years and though obviously there have been continuous evolutions in teas, methods and markets, there's a consistent pattern in both old and new. The harvesting and processing are focused on gently disturbing the stable structure of the leaf to release its compounds in waves that are in effect its distress signals to the rest of the plant: do something. This puts its stored compunds to work.

The teamaker Artisans use a wider range of ways to "fix" the leaf and stop its oxidation than Japanese ones: steaming, baking, woks and ovens. They allow more time in the withering and fixing and direct the searing heat way above boiling point – 300-400 degrees Fahrenheit and as high as 1,200. This creates unique sugary compounds called glucosides. The slower processing first releases the light and fresh lemony and grassy aromas and then the fuller vegetal aromas.

For tea drinkers, this has some clear impacts. The first is that

China greens are intendedly light, sugary and vegetal. The main differences among them are adding "very" to an adjective: very light, very sugary. For you, it may be too light, etc.

The second implication follows directly. For tea drinkers who are used to black teas, the China green taste and flavor profile can be hard to adjust to. The Japanese style produces darker, unsugary though more vegetal teas that are a closer match to their experience and preferences.

Pi Lo Chun: light and flowery

Pi Lo Chun means "green snail spring" and refers to the spiral shape of the leaves. It is mild and can seem too insipid for lovers of more forceful blacks and oolongs. But give it a few extra seconds in your mouth and you'll find an expansive and slightly crisp flavor that is very satisfying. It absorbs the flavor of fruit trees planted between the bushes; apricots are the main ones.

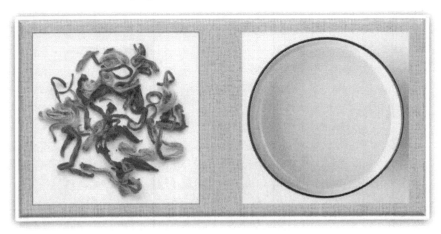

Pi Lo Chun tastes as distinctive and fresh as it looks

The leaf is distinctive and noted for its long, wiry form. 150-200 *thousand* buds must be picked to make just one kilo of Pi Lo. The price for the top grades is high, as with all the top ten China teas, but there's such a wide range of grades that it's easy to find good deals. There are seven official categories; reckon to pay no more than $6 an ounce, 50 cents a cup, for a medium-high grade, with plenty of good buys in the $4 range. Taiwan produces a slighter richer Pi Lo Chun than the traditional China variety.

Pi Lo is fresh, sweet, light, aromatic and flowery, often with a slight smoky overtone. It's one of the subtlest teas on the market. The lightness allows some very complex flavors to come through. The adjective that most lovers of this tea use to describe it is "artichoke." That seems a useful and accurate summary. If you cook artichokes, you will recall the smell of the liquid in the pan.

This is a tea for lovers of the light and subtle. It's suggested in *Tea Tips* as a better initial tryout, ahead of Dragonwell, of a high-end China green. It seems just that little bit tastier and likely to appeal to most palates. It is a delight, with a soft lingering aftertaste. Check that the source of origin is listed as Jiangshu, China.

Jasmine teas: A scent of perfection

Many tea bag drinkers prefer flavored to plain teas, generally herbal and/or Earl Grey. It can be hard for them to let go of the expectation of a big fruity or flowery upfront jolt and let a subtler flavor unfold. Jasmine infused tea is a good choice here. It's at one end of a spectrum from the bold and fruity citrus bergamot flavor of Earl Grey to the soft scented aromatic infusions of jasmine, rose and osmanthus petals at the other end.

Jasmine Pearls look unusual: small balls of contrasting green leaf and white jasmine, almost woven together. They are infused with the scent of fresh petals added to the leaf, simply by placing them next to it during the drying process. These are truly fresh and not an essence or a dried blossom. It takes around four hours for the tea to absorb the jasmine scent, after which the petals are removed.

The process is repeated 2-3 times for ordinary grades and up to 10 for the best grades. The scented leaves are then rolled. The sequence may take a month; then the leaves are re-fired to remove any moisture, and the blossoms may be removed or left in the tea. The leaf is formed into small balls that are visually striking.

When the tea is brewed, just a few dozen pearls will expand to half a cup, unfolding their locked in flavors. It's something to have on hand because it is a great "mood" tea that every so often is just what you feel like in the afternoon, and it is one of the few teas that adds to light food.

Jasmine pearls: fresh, unbroken leaf, fresh unbroken petals

Jasmine teas will appeal to anyone who enjoys sweet and mellow flavors. There is a wide range of these delicately scented teas: Jasmine Pearls, Silver Needle jasmine white, Jade oolong, and Jasmine green. Indian Nilgiri and Darjeeling producers are using jasmine in their green teas in their search to enhance fine leaf rather than add taste to a so-so base.

A caution here, though; the delicacy is as critical as the scent. The jasmine can be a little too obstructive in the foreground of the taste. Some tea lovers report that they view pearls as an occasional rather than regular drink and that, perhaps like chocolate, you can have too much of a good thing.

Much of this relates to the grade and processing. The complex and gentle infusion process invites shortcuts that downgrade jasmine pearls from super to OK. Single- and double-petals offer a subtler scenting than multi-petal ones. Other factors that affect quality are the bud-petal ratio, how many times the jasmine and leaf are lightly baked to smooth the infusion and, of course, the tea leaf itself. Some low price jasmine greens, the most popular variety, are undistinguished.

Overall, though, a well-made whole leaf jasmine tea is a special pleasure. It encapsulates just about every feature of the great tea making tradition of China. Pick a tea you love – white, green, oolong, Fujian, Darjeeling, Earl Grey, Mao Feng, or Silver Needle. See if there's a jasmine prefix for one on offer by your favorite provider. Try it. You'll probably add it to your special stock. When a friend who disdains green teas visits, bring out the jasmine pearls.

Don't get diverted by nomenclature. The traditional name of the tea is Dragon Pearl, with variants of Dragon Phoenix and occasionally Imperial. These can imply that a seller's tea is especially selective or elite. Forget the Dragon. Look for a description of the region: Fujian is the most highly regarded and teas from its Fuding area are the overall best. Then check if this is a spring tea and how many times it is infused in the marriage of tea leaf and flower petal.

Ignore the poetry illustrated by an ad for Emperor's Jasmine Pearls: "little green rings with wisps of silver... a strong, almost intoxicating scent." More informative is where this China green is made: Okinawa, Japan. It's not at all bad but it is factory produced, not Artisan grown, and uses the "sanpin" leaf of China origin that is the base for all Okinawa teas. So, different Empire, different leaf, different taste. But same selling pitch as Fuding, Fujian jasmine pearls plus a poetry surcharge: the price is fifty percent higher than the $5-6 an ounce (40-50 cents a cup) you should expect to pay for a good quality one.

Huangshan Mao Feng: cloud and mist

Huangshan Mao Feng comes from the Yellow Mountains in Anhui Province. Anhui is known for great teas and for being the area where modern loose leaf tea was first developed. Their distinctive characteristic is a light sweetness. Black Keemun Mao Feng comes from the same region.

Mao Feng green is a "yun wu" tea: cloud and mist, grown at a location where there's a lack of sunlight most of the days when the bush is close to harvesting. The plucking is very selective: one bud plus one attached leaf, which is noted for the delicate furry silver hairs on the underside. The name translates to Yellow Mountain fur peak. All this changes the chemistry of the tea to create a smoother and sweeter flavor than other China greens of note, with no bitterness. It is mellow but with plenty of lingering aromas.

Huangshan Mao Feng: delicacy plus craft

All in all, this is the quintessential China green, with just about all the common best features. It's rated one of the top four of the Great Teas of China and very popular there. It is surprisingly inexpensive for such a pedigree name but it's worth paying a little extra to get an early spring Huangshan.

There are many Mao Fengs now farmed in Fujian, Sichuan, Yunnan and other provinces. They are generally well made and the price is fair but while the bush and processing methods may transfer, the terrain doesn't. You can see the differences in the leaf. The Huangshan is noted for its long, whole and bright appearance. The others mostly lack the crisp and clean shape.

The China greens suggested here are not likely to be ones you drink in the morning, on the fly when commuting, or in the office.]

Japanese teas: as different as sushi and burgers

Here are a few Japanese green teas. Unless you are a devotee and/or visitor to Japan, you might not even recognize the powder and whisk on the left and the twigs in the middle as even being tea, let alone high grade, high rated ones, or that the bowls contain some of the most refined Japanese greens.

The powder is matcha, the twigs are kukicha, and the bowl contains sencha varieties. Japan is the only major tea producer that has been able to apply mechanization across the full harvesting and processing sequence without loss of quality. That's driven by labor and land scarcity.

Japanese teas: style and refinement. Definitely not English high tea Assam in a pot

Few of all these are exported. US and European supermarkets and grocery stores rarely display even tea bags and most tea drinkers will only have come across Japanese basic green as a side accompaniment to a restaurant meal. As well as unfamiliarity, there are good reasons not to buy Japanese teas, almost all of which are greens:

They are hard to shop for: Suppliers are relatively scarce; so many varieties, names, styles; senchas that look the same and are very different; unusual additions, not additives, to the finished tea, including popped rice and seaweed.

Brewing is a challenge: They almost all require lower temperatures and shorter times – 1-2 minutes – than other greens. Get this wrong and they can be undrinkable.

They go stale quickly: Five-day-old sushi? Not exactly a delicacy and not the most fun way to get food poisoning. Japanese teas are noted for their freshness. Suppliers ship them in vacuum packs or well-sealed laminated envelopes.

Once opened they lose their extra zip and quickly get flat.
They can be expensive: Cheap sencha isn't worth bothering
with: flat and boring. Expect to pay $5-8 an ounce for good
varieties (40-75¢ a cup), and $12 an ounce on up for
gyokuro. That said, there are quality Kukichas and
Houjichas for 30¢. (But if you want to try shincha, the first
harvest sencha, reckon on $20 an ounce (around $2 a cup.)
Some of them are weird: Matcha is a powder, much loved
but also disliked, and used as an ice cream flavor. Whisking
it is an art, let alone preparing it for the elaborate tea
ceremony.

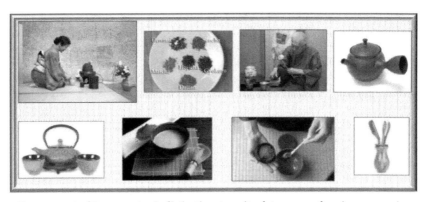

Every aspect of Japanese tea is distinctive: tea, ritual, tea ware, farming, processing

Tea Tips suggests that you try just three of the many options, ones
that are soft, pleasant and light but without any grassy, vegetal or
bitter flavors, that are easy to brew, and in the 40-50 cents a cup
price range. There are others that you may find even more enjoyable
– or are put off by. Kumbucha kelp tea is one instance. If you enjoy
raw fish, why not fermented seaweed? Many tea drinkers rave about
gyokuro and Matcha but they are costly and tricky to brew.

These ones are very approachable and may well motivate you to
try more exotic others: *Uji sencha*, one of the best of the many
regional varieties of the main Japanese green tea; *houjicha*, a soft
and smooth tea that is particularly suited to a relaxing pre-sleep
drink; and *kukicha*, a truly eccentric's notion of tea: it's made from

twigs but has a wholly tea flavor and aroma that are very satisfying.

They make an excellent contrast with the China greens discussed above. You may well find that they become an anchor taste for your choice of lighter teas. The main challenge is that they demand careful brewing: about half the time of other greens.

The central focus in Japanese tea making has been to produce an aromatic, almost scented drink. This makes freshness so essential. The aormas fade first. Senchas and gyokuro lose their expansive flavor more quickly than other teas. The delicacy of the steaming and shaping create a leaf that is vulnerable to higher temperatures and overlong steeping. You must decide if they are worth the effort.

The distinctive feature of Japanese green teas is the small, needle shape of the leaf and the brightness of the steamed ones. Processing manipulates chlorophyll through sun-shading.

Uji sencha: beautifully balanced

Sencha amounts to three quarters of the tea grown in Japan. When it is good it is superb. But there are wide variations in just about every element of its production. It's one of three main gradations, rather than grades. The lowest is bancha, where the leaf is from the two late harvests and lacking the sweetness and tenderness of the two spring and early summer ones. The highest is gyokuro, which is incomparable among teas, not necessarily the very best but in its own contrasting style from Chinese and Indian bests. Its name translates as "jewel dew", an accurate term for its sweetness and fresh, lively sense of an afternoon meadow.

There is a corresponding worst in this gradation. Avoid konacha; this is restaurant tea made of leftover dust from making senchas and gyokuro, waste that would otherwise be dumped. It is more of a cleansing agent than a beverage. Sushi and sashimi contain oily fish that leaves a coating in the mouth.

The Tea *Tips* suggestion that you pick Uji sencha is because it provides an anchor point for viewing the broad range of choices. Uji is a megamountain brand, the oldest tea producing region in Japan, near Kyoto. It's where the gentle steaming process that distinguishes sencha production was invented.

There are many outstanding senchas from other regions, such as Kagoshima and Shizuoko, with their distinctive climate-influenced variations, and many different styles: shade-grown kabuse, first-picked shincha, light-steamed akamushi, heavy-steamed fukamushi, and others.

All in all, Uji varieties are consensually rated as the most special in their depth of flavor; so many aromas, tastes and nuances are apparent and in perfect balance. Uji tea is aromatic, with a slight and pleasing sweet sense of new-mown grass but augmented by an offsetting nutty fullness.

The cliché about something "growing on you" seems not quite applicable to senchas. It is more a matter of do they grab you? An Uji sencha is a good test of this. If they do, then, yes, they may well grow on you, as you explore other varieties, such as the Kagoshima region's umidori sencha, very intense and a bright emerald green, or its kabuse sencha that is shaded from the sun for the last two weeks before harvesting.

You won't get any grab reaction from mediocre sencha. Japanese domestic demand has encouraged the importation of much lower quality Chinese sencha and factory blending that is above tea bag level, but not much.

Houjicha: inexpensive and toasty

This is a very smooth tea with no bitterness. It is roasted at a high temperature that changes the leaf from green tints to red. This results in a very clean taste, light and with a gentle toasty flavor. It is one of the teas that go well with food and is often recommended as a nighttime drink, just before going to sleep. The roasting cuts out many of the catechins that give green teas their sweet and grassy flavors and overlays them with a non-astringent toasty, almost caramel taste.

Houjicha is surprisingly inexpensive. It's an ingenious use of mainly lower quality bancha – "common tea" that is the produce from the last and least nutrient-rich harvest of the tea. One of the main purposes here is simply to level the growing fields in preparation for the spring. Japan's lack of natural resources has led to just about every element of its farming, cuisine and manufacturing being historically built on avoiding waste and using every part of ingredients.

Houjicha is an heir of this tradition. It is a technique which roasts bancha (and sometimes sencha) that often contains stems and twigs in porcelain pots over a charcoal fire. Not surprisingly, some reviewers describe it as having a slight mesquite flavor.

Check for quality: "Japanese" tea should not be marked "Made in China"

Houjicha is growing in popularity outside Japan. In general, Japanese mid-range teas are excellent quality. Low-end ones can be less than stellar. Stick with the megamountain and buy Uji houjicha.

Watch out for mass farmed China versions, as shown in the right-hand image above.

Kukicha: smoky, full enough, smooth

This tea fits the offbeat and quirky profile of Japanese teas. It breaks all the rules. First, forget two leaves and a bud: it's made from stems and twigs. It comes in shades of green and of brown. And it is as pleasant a tea as you could find anywhere.

There are two types of kukicha: a non-roasted steamed green and the suggested roasted one. The green is creamy and the roast one nuttier and fuller in flavor. Both are mellow and free of grassiness.

Green and roasted kukicha; both good, roasted better

The processing is selective and sophisticated. Tea plant branches are dried, aged for two years, steamed and most then gently roasted. Electrostatic driers are often used to create a magnetic effect that separates out the most desirable twigs and stems, with automated color recognition. These then go through four separate roastings in wood fired, iron cauldrons. This slowly builds the distinctive kukicha flavor and aroma. It is at the same time light with little sharpness or "green" vegetal/seaweed overtones but also full enough to have character, with its nutty near caramel body.

This selection of Japanese teas opens up a wide range of choices that are very different in flavors from the mainstream Chinese tradition. That makes them worth exploring if you are not a green tea enthusiast. Finding good suppliers is a slight problem and an ironic one. Japan is not a major tea exporter and few specialty tea stores stock even a small variety. Too many of the online offers are from packagers and you need to scan to locate the specialty sellers.

The irony is that for almost a century, Japan was the major supplier of US teas, after Commander Perry sailed his naval flotilla into Edo Bay in 1852 and made his Godfather-like offer that the shogunate could not refuse. This opened major trade routes and the decline of the whaling industry offered new opportunities to haul bulk cargo across the Pacific. World War II killed all that off.

The taste for Japanese teas has been largely lost in the West and many tea lovers will have encountered it only as a freebie alternative to an often more palatable glass of water. It really is worth trying the three suggestions. They may grab you. Then at some point you will sample gyokuro. Then there's no going back.

Moroccan mint: a refreshing change

The final suggested green tea for your exploration is outside the two mainstreams: India/Sri Lanka black teas and China/Japan greens. We naturally tend to stay within the boundaries of the style we know best. So, for instant, US and European shoppers will range across the black teas of India and the greens of China, but not the mint greens of North Africa. The chais of India are growing in global popularity but they are not yet embedded in the supply chains of the major brands.

One simple test of the mainstream is the selection of tea bags you find in an airport lounge, hotel self-service breakfast buffet, or office refreshment corner. It will always include the basic English Breakfasts and Earl Greys, plus flavored green and black teas and a few herbal ones. What is missing here is tea from the largest of all global tea traditions: the Arabic world.

The country with the highest per capital tea consumption is not England, but Turkey, where the average is over 3,000 cups per person per year, nine a day. Morocco is in second place, at five, followed by Ireland and the Independent Islamic Republic of Mauritania, and only then the UK. So much for tea being "English."

Or black.

Of the top 30 consumer countries, 15 are in the Middle East and North Africa, which now accounts for a quarter of global tea drinking. Tea is as much an Arabic as a European culture and as much influenced by Islam as Asia's was by Buddhism. This obviously doesn't fit the stereotypes of tea. How much does the average tea drinker or even the experienced Assamophile or Oolongist know about Turkish, Iranian or Moroccan teas?

This is a little ironic in that the several of these are attractive choices for tea drinkers whose anchor tastes are for flavored and floral drinks and who would like to find a healthy and palatable green tea. Moroccan mint is inexpensive and excellent in this regard. It combines the attractive piquant appealing fresh taste of spearmint with Chinese gunpowder tea, a low-cost green rolled into small pellets, mostly by machine.

The processing keeps the aroma locked in. Moroccan mint takes well to sugar or to drinking plain. It's inexpensive and easy to buy. It is a flavored tea that doesn't depend on additives and extracts.

Gunpowder green dates back to the Tang dynasty of the 7th to 9th century. It was supposedly later named for the resemblance to the pellets used in British cannons. It became the most common tea imported by Britain during the 18th century. Rolling preserved the life of the tea, reduced the breaking of leaf and made it easy to ship; the journey from Canton to London could take up to a year.

It created the Moroccan and Turkish tea market. North Africa was a coffee culture, with Mocha the main trade port. The Crimean war with Russia cut off British trade routes and left merchants with cargo loads of gunpowder green. Shipped to Tripoli and along the North African coast they created yet another set of national addictions to tea. It became and largely remains pervasive across the cultures as a core of hospitality, the ubiquitous tea houses, and the ceremonials.

Moroccan green tea with mint. Poured from a height to foam it.
Tea houses at the center of everyday society and a mark of hospitality.

Gunpowder is no longer a major component of the tea market. Few of the major brands sell it. It's not an interesting tea. But it's a good base for peppermint and the two offer a pleasant and fresh balance. While many of the Earl Grey, flowery pot pourri and fruit salad bags can be unsubtle, have a chemical tasting edge and overpower the palate, Moroccan mint is just a satisfying, clean tasting, smooth and fresh brew. It is also a distinctive complement or alternative to your everyday mainstream black or green teas. You may find it a welcome new taste to add to your occasional or even regular favorites.

White tea: processed by sunlight

White teas are an aristocratic cousin of green teas. Greens are lightly oxidized and gently heated. Whites are unoxidized and left undisturbed to wither naturally, up to three days versus a few hours for greens. This is practical only with buds that are plump and high in glucose.

Whites really should be part of your portfolio. They are too light to make a satisfactory daily breakfast wake up jolt, can be overpowered by rich foods, and are towards the high end of the price scale. But if you get hooked by them they are the perfect comfort drink. The best are as good as tea gets. This has always been a showcase special: scarce, exquisite and displaying the best of the craft. The most outstanding came from Fujian Province in China and from Sri Lanka, whose Adams Peak is one of the highest rated teas of any type.

The three classic China whites: Silver Needle, White Peony, Shou Mei.

Supply is expanding. There are now excellent white Darjeelings, good varieties from other China provinces, and some fine ones from Vietnam, Malawi, Nilgiri, Nepal and Kenya and even Hawaii. These teas are worthy of inclusion in the showcase. Some are more the equivalent of "homemade style", not quite the real thing but offering its main features. They include many lightly flavored teas that are a little greenish and lack some of the delicacy of the pure whites, though sharing their floral characteristics.

The simple answer to the question "*What* is white tea?" is that it's a variant of green teas but minimally processed without any heating or rolling, so that the leaves remain closest to their natural state. This retains the freshness and richness of the nutrients.

In many ways, there's no such thing as white tea. It name carries no legal weight or agreed on industry definition. It is distinguished less by what it is but by *how* it is made and *why* this differs from green tea production. This difference is analogous to that between "champagne" as a type of drink and the "méthode champenoise", which is the traditional one of four main ways of making sparkling wines. "Champagne" on a label doesn't tell you much about the nature or quality of the drink; it's the method that differentiates it.

Showcase white teas come from what might be termed the "méthode Fujian" of minimalist precision. It's a way of "making" tea based on just let it be: Harvest the very best buds during the shortest period, and do as little to it as possible.

The plucking shows the minimalism and points to its cost. It lasts for just a single week or two in the spring, less than days before the buds unfold into a leaf; they are packed with nutrients built up during the winter. Harvesting stops if there is any rain, dew or frost. Only buds that have a full shape and long length are selected.

The main variety of bush is unique for the downy white hairs on the buds that evolved to protect against bugs. The plants provide a jolt of glucose that makes them sweeter than maturing leaves. They also add a boost of extra caffeine and the antioxidants that are believed to give tea medical powers of prevention and cure.

The minimalism is pervasive. Nothing is done to the leaf beyond letting it wither in the air. The tea is not allowed to oxidate – in theory, though practice varies for some non-showcase names. It simply lightly dries. It is meticulously inspected to ensure that the final leaf is uniform in size and shape and unblemished.

There's some fine-tuning in this traditional process, which produces the Silver Needle white tea that is a peak of the Artisan craft, with distinctive characteristics of wide appeal. It is surprisingly full while also delicate, so that its flavors expand in your mouth. It is subtle and smooth with a hint of sweetness and no astringency. The flavor is floral, whereas comparable lighter green teas tend to be vegetal, with a grassy aroma.

It is robust, too, and more tolerant of temperature and time in brewing than greens. Its flavors are strong enough for you to just let them unfold but light enough for any one of them to become dominant. Some people do find it watery. It doesn't demand an expert palate but more a sense of the palette of tea tastes built from experience.

Silver Needle (Yin Zhen) has pride of place in the showcase. Alongside are Eyebrow (Shou Mei), and White Peony (Bai Mu Dan). They ease away from minimalism. White Peony adds the two leaves below the bud, for instance

China, Silver Needle: closing in on perfection

Silver Needle or Yin Zhen is almost a generic global name for one of the very best white teas, originally from China but with some excellent varieties from Sri Lanka and even Darjeeling. They are all at the extreme of lightness and lowest in caffeine of the great teas. To a large degree, you won't go wrong buying any of them. The price varies quite widely, with many gourmet options. $7-8 an ounce offers the best balance between quality and price.

The name comes from the silvery, tiny hairs on the underside of the leaf and the shape of the tea leaves after processing; they are a silvery green and look like small needles. The liquor from the brew is a very light lemony color that may appear almost tasteless. The trick is to pluck the bud just before it opens and begins its unfurling. Some whites add a few very new leaves that have just started to open.

White tea emerged late in the long history of Chinese tea growing. Silver Needle was first produced commercially in 1885 and White Peony in 1922. It has always been localized, specialized, and small in scale, and this is reflected in the techniques and variety of producers. It is not a high volume, mass market item like black teas. One element of the specialization is the type of tea plant. There are three of these from which China whites are made: Big White leaves, Narcissus White and Vegetable White.

Silver Needle is the highest grade of "silver tip" whites that come from the Big White variety of leaf. There is an atmosphere of poetic reverence about silver tips: "White like cloud, green like dream, pure like snow, aromatic like orchid." Yeah, sorta.

Leaves left over from the production of Silver Needle and White Peony, a slightly stronger silver tip tea, are used to make other very good teas such as Long Life Eyebrow. There is a slightly herbal taste to them. They are all fresh and clean in their flavor. The word "delicate" most accurately captures this.

The processing is extremely selective and careful. The leaves will be plucked only under very strict conditions: never on rainy days or when the morning dew has not dried, never when the buds are purple, open, too long or too thin, affected by insects, or there is frost on the ground. The withering is equally selective. If the conditions are too hot, the leaves will become reddish and if they are too cold then they will blacken. The buds must be the youngest on the plant and picked before they open.

White Peony: Light, a touch of woodiness

White Peony is a silver tip white tea that is just a little stronger in flavor than Silver Needle. It is also known as Pai Mu Dan. It is made in parallel with Silver Needle, using the buds with two tip leaves that remain after the ones chosen for the Silver Needle have been plucked. Whereas the liquor for Silver Needles is a pale yellow, that of White Peony is more of a light brownish gold. It has an additional hint of a smoky, roasted "mushroomy" aroma.

This is a popular tea, grown in several China provinces. They vary in the proportion of tips and maturity of the leaf. It's a bridge between light and vegetal greens and subtle Silver Needle whites.

Four White peonies, differing bud amounts and young/mature leaf

Shou Mei: Less bud, more body

Shou Mei is the preferred choice of many tea drinkers because it is a little fuller and bolder in taste. It's almost a light oolong.

The leaf form of Shou Mei is the most common; there's not much reason to seek out the cake.

Shou Mei is inexpensive and often discounted, largely because it's made from the less selective parts of the leaf. There's a strong case for making it a first choice; the extra aroma and body plus the price are a standout combination.

Nor is grade here equivalent directly to quality. White teas differ in terms of how much bud they are made from in relation to leaf. Silver Needle is the first spring plucking, leaving fewer buds for White Peony which is one bud for each two leaves. Shou Mei is left with fewer tips and buds and is made from the remaining more mature and larger leaves. It comes in various forms of cake and is often marketed under its cumbersome Chinese name, Longevity Eyebrow, a reference to the shape of the leaf.

All three categories of these white teas are an excellent buy in terms of value for money. Silver Needle is, unsurprisingly, the highest priced. Expect to pay close to $8 an ounce. Two ounces will last months, well-stored. This is not an everyday breakfast tea but one for evenings or a quiet interlude. Good White Peony is in the $5-7 range and Shou Mei a little less.

Moonlight sonatas: the great white teas

There's one category of white teas that are in the $15-20 range. "Moonlight white" tea draws the same sighs respectful silence as the last notes of a beautiful piana sonata. It's a proud announcement by respected tea growing communities in China's Yunnan and Fujian plus a small number of estates in Sri Lanka and Darjeeling.

| Yunnan Moonlight teas | Ancient tree | Moonlight brick |

Moonlight whites are the quintessence of selectvity and refinment, from the growing, timing of harvesting, and handling. They are one of the showcase teas of the world.

The message adds up to: "This is as good as white tea can get. It's made of the very, very best leaf through equally outstanding and accomplished methods. Every detail and step is immaculate." It implicitly adds "And it's gonna cost you."

The Chinese term is believed to refer to the tradition in Yunnan of harvesting the buds under the light of the moon, to capture them at their most tender, with a little moisture on the bushes; around 30% will be unopened, concentrating the subtle aromas that are a hallmark of Moonlights. The more buds, the higher the quality. The better the leaf, the more the underside will show a light downy fur, almost whispy.

It is always hard to describe subtle flavors and tea talk can get very convoluted, high flown and adjective-drunk. Perhaps the best word to use here is "vaguely." The tea is vaguely sweet, with a vaguely floral aroma. It's a wealth of shifting hints slightly/lightly/leaning to spicy and so on.

At the same time, it is surprisingly full in taste. One useful review summarizes the Darjeeling Castleton estate's near legendary Moonlight White second flush as: "Floral/herbaceous profiles with a sweet top note thing going on."

Four Darjeeling Moonlight whites: Thurbo, Badamtam, Jungpana, Margaret's Hope

Each Artisan region making whotes exploits the distinctive characteristics of terrain and tradition. Darjeeling ones are a different leaf style and slight;y bolder flavor.

Obviously, Moonlight white is not a tea to drink on a regular basis, but if you like tea and are due a birthday present... This is one that you really should try once... or twice. Maybe start with a medium grade White Peony; this costs little more than a high end teabag. Move up to Silver Needle and then try a Darjeeling Thurbo,

Badamtam or Margaret's Hope, the even higher rated Castleton, Makaairabi and Jungpana, a highland Sri Lanka Needle and the sublime Adams Peak... They are all worth a splurge.

Complex crafted teas: Oolongs, Puehrs

Black and green teas constitute the main superhighways of the global industry, from bush to cup. These are relatively easy to travel in terms of finding teas and outlets, with plenty of stops along the way. There are other Interstates that offer plenty of scenic panoramas and side roads. Two of these are worth your exploring. Either of them may well become your main travel route:

Oolongs: Oolongs span a wide spectrum of tastes between black and green teas. They amount to under 2% of US tea sales, largely because they do not fit the production and distribution priorities of the global retail brands. They are highly individualized in their processing, which is labor-intensive and lengthy. One blogger summarizes them as the most "chefy" of teas.

Puehrs: This is a black tea distinguished by its forms as well as its taste. You use a sharp tool such as a knife or even a screwdriver to chisel pieces off leaf compressed into many shapes and sizes. Puehrs age superbly, up to centuries in some noted instances and their "raw" and "cooked" varieties are earthy, smoky and redolent of flavors. They are tricky to shop for, with many fakes and cons.

Oolongs include some of the world's very best teas and there is surely one(s) out there for you. Puehrs are a taste that once acquired is inexhaustible in the range and complexity of options.

Oolongs: the art of the tea master

Oolong teas are processed to produce complexity of flavor. You can find one that has the main characteristics of the green or of the black teas you like but with an additional something that is appealing. For example, the great Taiwan high mountain oolongs are lighter than blacks but with an extra almost smoky richness. Jade oolongs are a rich, smooth floral accentuation of the flavors of first rate green teas.

The range of oolongs is shown in the examples of leaves below.

This largely reflects the degree to which the leaf is oxidated. The oolong process preserves the richness of the leaf but removes bitterness. The "fixing" stage is central, with the timing of manual pan-steaming stopping further oxidation. It involves between ten and twenty steps that are meticulously timed and fine-tuned to the characteristics of the batch of harvested leaf.

Oolongs are shaped carefully to store and unfold their individual flavors

Very roughly, the processing begins as if this were a black tea and then the fixing switches to green tea operations and ends with the leaf bang heated to bring out its individual flavor.

Here's a *Tea Tips* prediction. If you are a tea lover, you will over time become an oolong zealot. That's regardless of whether you start out only drinking black teas or greens. That's because the chef-like craft of the tea master can tease out so much complexity in the leaf and make it in tightly curled, twisted and compacted forms that let it expand and release its flavors gently. This is a tea that grows on you; it exercises the palate. You can pick ones close to green or to black.

There are three main styles of oolong, immediately visible from their shapes. Flat leaf oolong is long and crinkly and processed to bring out sweetness and a springtime floral aroma. It was historically thought of as like a dragon's rippling scaled body and "oolong" translates to black dragon. You'll see ads for five dragon oolongs, grey, golden and orange, dragon eye and wood dragon. The wordplay is innocuous.

Balled oolong is the product of multiple around the clock, continuous rollings of the leaves, followed by tea-firing in woks, and baking. The finished tea looks like small, green dumplings with occasional attached stems. It is light and packed with lingering flavors. Taiwan's high mountain oolongs are balled.

Strip oolongs are the style for many China oolongs, including the best of the best: Da Hong Pao. They are darker and longer than open leaf ones and formed into long twists. They are heavily roasted to produce an earthy and pervasive flavor. They are the core of Wuyi rock oolongs.

One of the most distinctive features of oolongs is that they can be re-steeped several times, with each infusion a little different, generally softer and more mellow. The most famous and expensive Da Hong Pao – Big Red Robe – can be rebrewed more than ten times.

There are many oolongs, mainly Chinese but with Taiwan offering some of the most superb and Darjeeling and Nepal growers adding a Himalayan style to them. Four stand out as ones any tea lover must try:

Tie Guan Yin, known in English as Iron Goddess of Mercy. The classic oolong, widely available in varying grades and quality. Its reputation is slipping from its peak with the increase in low grade production via corner-cutting, high pesticide use and adulteration. The Chinese Tie Guan Yin comes from China's Anxi province. It is facing strong competition in reputation and excellence from the Taiwan ones, that are a little heavier, smokier and fuller than the greener Anxi.

Taiwan Alishan High Mountain oolongs and Dong Ding. Nutty, with many variations from the roasting times and repeats in processing. Alishan oolongs are setting the standard for fuller oolongs with a rich aromatic flavor.

Wuyi Da Hong Pao. Big Red Robe. The original Da Hong bushes provide the base for the luxury Da Hongs that cost thousands of dollars a pound. Growers have created less costly varieties that are still very good indeed.

The four teas are balls and strips and towards the high oxidation end of the scale. They are suggested for you to try because they very much fit most Western tea lovers' anchor tastes. One type of oolong that is excluded is Dan Cong, an open leaf tea from Guangdong Province in China. That is because it's harder to locate, very varied, complex to brew and more elusive in its tastes. It's more suited to green tea fans. But it is truly superb.

Here are images of the suggested oolongs plus Dan Cong, for reference:

Oolongs from China and Taiwan: layers of flavors, subtle and complex

Other excellent choices include milk oolong, ginseng, aged, smoked and regional specialties. For some reason, oolongs have attracted poetic and eccentric naming. Along with Iron Goddess, Big Red Robe and Oriental Beauty, there is a *yasha* oolong that is growing in popularity; this translates as Duck Shit, not found on the supermarket shelf. There's also White Cockscomb, Golden Water Turtle, Eastern Beauty and Water Fairy.

India's elite tea growers have added oolongs to their black tea base. Some are interesting but by and large they are very expensive and do not come close to the Taiwan ones. Start with Tie Guan Yin, the classic, and then go for an Alishan and Dong Ding.

The teas generally go by their generic identity, with no estate brands but many varieties of style, some whose names are commercial inventions of individual packagers. Mountain Copper oolong sounds special. It's from "India" and it gets some of the worst reviews of any tea outside a tea bag. Many state that it doesn't look, taste or smell like an oolong, and has no oolong flavor.

The only names that are of any relevance are where the oolong comes from and if it's one of the pedigree styles. Think of it as a way of making tea: very sophisticated, dependent on the nature of the soil and terrain, time-consuming and labor-intensive. The idea of an oolong blend is a self-contradiction. The label is misused even by the major brands. One of the top three global names markets its China Oolong Tea as a black tea "style" and oolong "flavor." It's an "ancient blend" of China black teas. Another global giant's oolong is blended and packaged in the USA. There is no reason whatever to buy these. None.

Anxi's Iron Goddess

Tie Guan Yin, the Chinese name that translates as Iron Goddess of Mercy, is the third best known name among all Chinese products, according to a survey of 2,600 business people from over 40 countries carried out by the China Brand Research Institute. It is a benchmark for oolongs. It's in the middle range, closer to a black than a green tea, but lighter and less astringent.

Tie Guan Yin is immediately recognizable from its tight rolled shape, common across its varieties.

The Anxi region in China's Fujian Province is the source of many oolongs. They are processed somewhat differently from other ones, including those from Taiwan: fermented for a shorter time and then baked for longer. The best summary of their special flavor is that an Anxi oolong has overtones of a rich honey taste that lingers well.

The Anxi oolong industry is unusual in that its producers and wholesalers do not classify the teas by leaf but by the quality of the final drink made from them. The highest grade is Fanciest and the lowest is Common. To get started, choose a Select or Fine Select from a reliable online supplier.

Iron Goddess is slightly expensive to buy but, that said, it can be resteeped several times, with each new infusion bringing out a new element of its flavor. It is fragrant and fills the mouth in the way that a great wine does. It begins with an almost bitter taste that takes your palate by surprise. As you sip it, it becomes a very light and floral flavor.

There are probably more adjectives thrown around in ads that describe it than for any other tea: it is toasty (true) and has hints of grain, figs (yeah, perhaps), orchid finish (eh?), roasty, luminous golden-orange (that probably makes sense to someone) and with buttery density (that doesn't). Even the appearance of the tightly twisted dark leaves gets praise. So, all in all, the best adjective may simply be "great."

It's one of the most easily located pedigree teas, with competitive prices that make it both excellent and affordable. There have been growing problems of quality control in China because of its popularity. Some producers are short-cutting the complex fine-tuning of the tea oolong process. Taiwanese Tie Guan Yins are often the best choice.

Taiwan Alishan High Mountain oolong

Alishan oolong is a mountain megabrand, named for one of the most outstanding tea growing regions of the world, in Taiwan. And one of the newest, dating back just a few decades when it was introduced by Chinese farmers.

The main ones come from the Zhi Zuo area of cooperative estates, all small and very individual in their teas. Alishans are noted for a mellow creamy flavor, with a floral fragrance. They are oxidated enough to provide a full body and the layers of citrus and flowers is rich and pervasive. These seem to be a lucky result of the elevation of the mountains plus the relative cold, which stunts the growth of the leaf enough to add these complexities.

Alishan tea gardens vary in terrain, size, terracing, etc.
What's constant is the cloud mist and the meticulous processing.

The processing is unusual and relies on sophisticated methods of rolling the leaf to remove the moisture in stages. The batches are rolled up to 30 times in a 6-8 hour period in canvas bags tied tight enough to catalyze the process without damaging the leaf. They are shaped into tight balls that concentrate the flavors and aromas.

It's hard to put a label on Alishans. They pack a wide range of flavors into an enticingly mellow smoothness. It seems fair to say that no other tea quite achieves that balance; they are more often marked by a planned imbalance: some element of flavor that stands out in the foreground of the taste experience.

Prices vary widely, because the tea is so much in demand, in both the foreign and domestic markets and it is not a standardized or large-scale farming produce. Most of the growers are smallholders with regional varieties – Zhong Su Hu, Shi Zuo – and in the leaf itself. Juan Xian leaf is cheaper than the Chinhsin cultivar and grows much faster; it is substantially less expensive and a good general choice.

Alishans offered for less than $6 an ounce, about 50 cents a cup, are unlikely to be from the gardens best located in terms of sunlight, soil and weather patterns. The ones at $20 an ounce – a hefty $1.50

– are stunningly good. Choose your supplier carefully and look for evidence of specialized contacts and expertise.

Dong ding

Dong Ding is one of the best of the Taiwan oolongs. It's medium-oxidated with a full. mellow body plus a floral sweetness – a lighter version of an Alishan one and indeed the original bush stock for those High Mountain oolongs. Known also as Tung Ting, the name translates to "frozen peak," It's one of the most satisfying of all teas.

Dong Ding is complex to make and some farmers are reducing the oxidation to simplify processing. That reduces oxidation and also the fullness of the flavors. The name is becoming generic and almost a style of tea. So, when you see an ad for a "Formosa" or even "Taiwan" Dong Ding, check the country of origin. It may well turn out to be Thailand or Vietnam. The best are from Natou County – in Taiwan, of course.

Da Hong Pao, Big Red Robe

The final suggested oolong, Da Hong Pao, Big Red Robe, is one of the most highly regarded of all teas. It's a Wuyi rock tea with a rich legendary history and an equally interesting real one. The Wuyi mountains in Fujian Province are full of steep cliffs, with mineral-rich soil, limestone, bamboos and rivers.

Tea bushes grow "defiantly" in the useful description in gaps in the boulders and in patches of garden nestled in the karst landscape. This is the term for a topography formed by the dissolution of soluble limestone, gypsum and dolomite, that results in strata marked by sinkholes, underground drainage, caves and chemical interactions that can generate sulfuric acid in the water, precipitation of calcium carbonates, and even disappearing lakes.

Such terrain is not conducive to human habitation. Sinkholes can suddenly emerge and caverns collapse. Groundwater is easily polluted. There are innumerable recorded reports of animals, homes, farm machines and in Oklahoma an entire museum being swallowed up.

Ignore the myths and mystique; enjoy the dark, multiflavored rock tea

All these factors have created one of the great environments for teas. Many of the bushes are centuries old and the leaf is packed with nutrients. The terrain remains unthreatened by development and large-scale farming. Tea growing and processing is small-scale and localized in villages. Da Hong Pao is a lucky accident, the best of what is more broadly known as Wuyi rock oolong.

The name comes from typical tea myth. A tea from Wuyi cured the sickness of a mother of a Ming dynasty Emperor, sometime between 1368 and 1644. He sent a big red robe to cover the four bushes from which it came. The local farmer continued to hoof up the cliff and send the tea as a gift to the far off Imperial court.

Regardless, there are six bushes from which all Da Hong Pao came. The cluster produced about a kilogram of tea a year. It also established prestige and price levels of absurd fame. These "mother tress" shown in the central image above were harvested up through 2005 and even today antique tea leaves are hoarded as treasures.

They may date back to 1300. In 2002, 20 grams, enough for four cups, sold for $28,000.

Since then, good grade Big Red Robe has been made from new clones of bush propagated from cuttings of the original. Second-generation ones are more highly prized than later offspring and siblings. Cheaper ones are more overroasted and other Wuyi leaf may be mixed in. The best is made very close to the cliff where the mother bushes still stand.

Puehrs: bricks, bowls and mushrooms

Puehrs account for a tiny fraction of the Artisan tea market. They are a compressed not loose leaf tea. All the shapes below are commonplace in puehr production.

Just a few of the many puehr shapes;
A leading online vendor's site lists a thousand items

Puehrs became in effect a trade currency, key to buying scarce horses from the mountain tribes in the Tibetan plateau. The still-traveled Old Tea Horse Road runs 3,000 mountainous miles from

Yunnan, where puehr remains predominantly made, to Bengal, Sichuan, Tibet and Burma. It is somewhat winding.

10,000 kilometers (6,000 miles); not one stop light; trading posts every 500 km or so

Flat bricks were easy to transport by caravan, bing disk platters stacked compactly with space to breathe and continue maturing, mushrooms were branded as being for the Tibetan market, and tuocha were small monetary change and probably strung together as a necklace. Puehrs often come baked in whole tangerine and tamarind peel, and tea coins are packed into bamboo tubes.

Squares are still formed with embossments of religious symbols, dragons, pagodas, horses, etc. Pumpkin-like and pumpkin-size melons were striped to mark them as tribute teas. (Larger ones were known as "Hunan-head" tea, to be presented at court in the same manner as gifts of the severed heads of rebels and rivals.)

The wrappers of puehrs are as varied as the shapes. They are made of thin cotton cloth or cotton paper and show the tea company name or factory, the year of production, the region/mountain of harvest, the plant type, and the recipe number.

A small ticket ("nèi fēi") indicating the tea factory and brand is now usually embedded into the cake during pressing. This is used as evidence of identity and authenticity. There is a widespread industry of knock offs made of lower quality leaf, not as aged as claimed or less carefully processed. A larger description ticket or flyer is packaged loose under the wrapper.

Puehr wrappers are a small data base of information and the baked in label its certification. These reflect the immense variety of puehrs

Recently, nèi fēi have become more important in identifying and preventing the frequent counterfeits. The famous Menghai Tea Factory has begun microprinting and embossing nèi fēi on the cake itself. (Fake puehrs illustrate their value and cachet: there's no comparable market opportunity in counterfeiting English Breakfasts.)

The contrasts between puehrs and Artisan black, green and white teas reflect the complex chemical composition of the leaf that can be manipulated in so many ways. The other types of tea cut off future changes in the finished leaf. Puehrs maintain an ongoing natural maturing, "fermenting" and aging their mix of leaves, including hardier and less tender ones than the buds that are so critical for making the other types. It's this that differentiates raw, aged raw and ripe puehrs.

A candidate puehr

Earl Grey tea is easy to find. Shopping for puehrs is not so simple. The tea doesn't come to you – you'll have to get to it. Finding puehrs in stores is more like treasure-hunting than shopping. Go online.

There really is little alternative. This is a specialty tea, that requires specialty knowledge on the part of buyer and seller, and specialty sourcing, pricing and quality control. Very few tea retailers know much about puehrs and will stock just a few, almost as a novelty item.

That said, if you calibrate your expectations and look for an affordable puehr from a site that has a fairly broad inventory, you'll easily find plenty of interesting options.

The photos shown below are from the author's stash of puehrs. In all, these took maybe two hours to locate, evaluate and buy, and 1-2 weeks to get delivery from two suppliers in China, two in the US and one in Canada. They amount to around four pounds of tea and cost maybe $150 – the same range as tea bag prices.

For yourself, these may look interesting as household decorations but a fair reaction is probably "Why would I want to buy that?" Or "That sounds interesting but I can't afford it." Or just "I don't know why I would even try it."

These live on in a display cabinet and have been left whole, instead of pieces being broken or chiseled off, simply because they are so attractive and intriguing.

There's a risk in buying puehrs, with many misrepresentations, adulterations, scandals, and low quality fakes. If you are interested in exploring the many hundreds of good ones, the *Tea Tips* advice is to ignore the *Tea Tips* advice. Find an expert.

But not a purist, unless you are willing to spend plenty of time and money on the obscurities of puehr types, flavors and pedigree. These are superb but complex to choose and to brew. Try a more ordinary one and see if you like the style. Here's an affordable and enjoyable example. It was bought online from a mall that offers many good deals, has a massive variety of products, and ensures fast and generally free delivery. You may well have heard of it: eBay. The seller is a first-rate specialist in Hong Kong that uses eBay as its storefront.

A caffeinated Frisbee? Compacted mulch? About 150 cups of tea, anyway.

This bing is middle level in quality and price. It is not a luxury item. It was made in a factory that mainly offers younger puehrs – five years or less. Many purists argue that a puehr needs fifteen years to be fully ready for drinking.

Puehrs are the only teas that benefit from aging. The problem for most other whole leaf ones is the opposite need, for freshness. Japanese teas in particular need coddling and a good many of the best tea sellers are vacuum packing their teas to ensure extra prevention of staleness. The rule of thumb is that, properly stored, Artisan teas will remain fresh for around a year.

A puehr that young aren't worth even considering. Occasionally, one turns up that is a few hundred years old and still ripening. High end ones are sometimes recooked after a decade or so.

When puehrs have been mentioned in the press, it has generally been because of the astonishing prices for old and rare ones. These became a fad in Hong Kong, rather like collecting wines from Jefferson's cellar. Prices multiplied tenfold in 2007, then crashed. But one piece still sold for close to $2 million in 2013, for just two *ounces.* The bubble burst in the early 2000s but there are still many on offer for several thousand dollars. eBay's 2015 listings included a 1940s shu for just $19,101 (free shipping).

Historically, puehr has been the preserve of Yunnan Province. Other regions in China, Burma, Vietnam and Laos produce varieties but those of the Six Great Mountains of Yunnan and Xishuangbana, the center of puehr history, stand out in every regard: terrain, methods, skills, and even the ancient and wild trees it is made from.

Xidai: mountains, history, culture, diversity, temples, tea.
Many of the megamountain tea regions are tourist heavens and havens.

Mentioning "Xishuangbana" in a real estate listing is equivalent to "Yunnan Province: warm, humid, isolated, tropical biodiversity; monsoons May through October." Not an attractive place for retirement, developing a software company or opening a restaurant. But for making puehrs, Xidai (the abbreviation) is the tea equivalent of a zip code like 94027, which is where Silicon Valley gazillionaires reside. Here, the residents are poor but their products stellar.

Xidai offers wild forest trees, as old as 150 years and up to 20 feet high, shared by the village community in a completely protected environment. It is the home of the famous Menghai tea factory that set the standards and developed the methods for making raw puehrs in the 1970s and 80s.

The tea in this example is a Huang Dian, which means "yellow leaf." (Apparently, it is also slang for "porn movie." Chinese tea terminology does pose some special problems.)

Whereas almost all the traditional china teas are made from the famous "two leaves and a bud" puehrs use the bigger third and fourth leaf. These grow on plants that are not kept trimmed but allowed to spread in the wild and reach heights of 10-20 meters, with some claimed to be a thousand years old.

The leaf is carefully selected – by hand, of course. The best goes to the factory to make the higher grade puehrs. The yellow leaves are "farmers' choice" meaning that they are what the growers drink and less commercially marketed.

Puehrs are noted for their earthy flavor, which in tea that has been made from good leaf and properly fermented and aged, is smooth and full. They don't have the boldness and tippiness of black teas but are far bigger in the mouth than greens and oolongs.

One of their most distinctive elements is that they can be rebrewed many times and that rather than losing flavor they take on more and more "notes" as a new pot is made from the same leaves. You break a piece from the cake – one measure of quality is that the leaves should be of consistent size and appearance across the whole piece.

This one is a relatively low end grade. There are hundreds better, but even so it's in a different league from even superior black tea blends. It doesn't have any intrusive notes: very smooth, not too smoky or earthy, and pleasant to sip. The second and third infusions add mellowness. Later ones preserve the taste and extend the softness.

Obviously, a tea such as this Huang Pian must be far harder to find that either the leading branded blends or most commonly stocked loose leaf teas. It is a specialized variety of a specialized tea that most people have never heard of or seen. And obviously, it will be relatively expensive. It has no solid distribution base: how many puehrs have you yourself ever seen let alone tasted?

"Obviously" turns out to be the wrong word. Puehrs are easy to find online. The prices range from cheaper than tea bags to ultra-costly for the scarcest and oldest: fine jewelry level payouts.

Here are just a few figures on availability:

Amazon: These are late-2016 search results: "Puehr tea" 2,027 items, "Aged puehr" 621, "Puehr brick" 234, "Puehr cake" 717.

One of the best known online puehr specialty stores based in China lists over 800 teas, in the range of $15-300.

eBay: There are about 5,000 listed either for auction or "buy now."

Another highly rate online tea provider lists around 250 puehrs with a median price of $30 for 12 ounces – that's equivalent to around 15 packages of tea bags. It makes the high end puehr cost far less than half that for commodity bags and blends.

The Huang Pian puehr cost $23, with free shipping from China, in late 2015. The tea cake is 357 grams, the standard size for a bing cake: 12.6 ounces. At the average conversion rate of 12 cups per ounce and assuming just two infusions (four is more typical), that amounts to 300 cups – 7 cents each.

Compare this with the good quality tea bags or a comparable loose leaf blend at around 25 cents. This Huang Pian costs just 7 cents a cup for a far more flavorful, smooth and satisfying drink. Even if you don't add a second infusion, this Artisan choice costs less than the best on the supermarket shelf. Puehrs are a bargain.

They can be a luxury, too. Amazon lists twelve at over $1,000 for 4 to 12 ounces. The general advice from regular tea drinkers is to avoid the really cheap teas – the best price/taste value seems to be in the range of $12 for four ounce bricks and $40 for twelve ounce cakes.

The issue for *Tea Tips* is not to rate puehrs but simply to point out that they are out there and easily accessible and to dismiss any notion that whole leaf tea is special, luxury and expensive. It isn't, unless it's made so by marketing and packaging.

Tea and living well

What we really know

More than any other beverage, the tea market is very much driven by broad lifestyle interests that shape what drinkers look for and how providers position products and accessories. These interests include the social experiences of afternoon tea, Japanese tea ceremonies, and gongfu rituals. Pots, tea sets, cream cakes and tea sandwiches add to its evocative associations. The product positioning builds on a long tradition of elegant and artistic design of porcelain, silver tea sets and historical trappings that extends to superb modern packaging. All these add to the tea experience.

More general and substantive lifestyle factors are the health aspects of tea as an element in well-being: the belief that it has powerful preventative and curative powers for almost every major disease, helps the body lose weight and cleanses the system. Counterforces seen as negatives are caffeine, pesticides and the gap between organic and mass farming methods.

Much of all this is taken as a given. That is most apparent in the general assumption that green tea has significant *medicinal* powers, including in being *lower* than other teas in *health-damaging caffeine*. All the highlighted words in that last sentence are not correct. The accurate restatement is: Green tea has no scientifically proven medical powers of any type or degree. It is on average lower in caffeine that other teas but often higher, and it makes no difference in term of the impact of caffeine, which is not a health risk, except for a very small fraction of the population.

Treating the tea-health link as "everyone knows" often means choosing teas that taste truly awful, are overpriced, and don't do you any good. The reason to drink tea is because it's enjoyable. If enjoyment includes brewing it in an elegant pot or in an automated tea machine, great. If you like green tea or avoid it, your option. If you are happy sticking with tea bags, well, it's your constitutional right. But if you base your decisions about what to drink on well-being and that really matters for you, then you need to get beyond the "everyone knows" conventional — often little more than folk — wisdom.

Tea Tips offers a briefing on what we know about the tea/well-being links. You must obviously make your own assessments about the weight you place on the claims and evidence. Overall, it does seem likely that tea is a desirable element of your diet. Given that, it makes sense to view Artisan tea, additive-free and naturally processed from quality leaf, as correlative with good health but not necessarily causal.

Does tea cure cancer or prevent diabetes? No

The scientific research is clear: there is just no evidence to support claims about tea's medical powers, only occasional and suggestive hints. That does not mean that they should be dismissed, just that tea is a drink, not a medicine. It may well be that it does have positive health powers, making this another reason to choose it over caffeine or soda but don't in any way count on it directly helping you lose weight, prevent cancer or cure diabetes. Just enjoy your drink.

Here's a summary of the composite picture that emerges from the scientific studies of the lifestyle impacts of tea:

> *Tea has not been proven* to make significant *direct* impacts on any aspect of health. It does not *directly* help drinkers lose weight. There is not a single study among many thousands that shows a statistically significant, replicated connection.

> Even after fifty years of research, just about every peer-reviewed paper is packed in its conclusions with "may", "suggests", "possible" and further study is needed." There are many fundamental problems of methodology, measurement, isolation of interrelated causes and effects, sample characteristics, time frames, etc.

> *The risks of caffeine* affecting mood, sleep, body stability, etc., are for most of the population very low. The belief that green and white teas are lower in caffeine than black ones is incorrectly based on out of date average figures; individual

types of tea vary widely in caffeine milligrams per serving.

Pesticides and contaminants seem to be under control for teas exported from Asia and Africa, though a growing number of low grade ones contain heavy lead absorbed from the soil; some surveys estimate that 75% are above the recommended safety limits, though both the figures and risks are open to question.

The European Union and Japan have tight inspection rules and processes and China has strengthened its notoriously weak oversight of agriculture. In the US, oversight of tea has been complicated by its being marketed as food produce, as a beverage and as a dietary and health supplement, all of which involve many agencies and regulations – and battalions of lobbyists who have for instance successfully blocked restrictions on tea supplements.

The terms "natural" and "organic" are not as clear an indicator of quality and purity as the terms suggest. Many herbal teas and tea supplements are far more dangerous than standard brands and tea types, to the extent that they represent a significant danger to health.

Interactions between ingredients and medications are unpredictable and gaps in regulation and oversight substantial. There are routine reports and warnings of green and herbals tea causing heavy damage to liver and kidneys when used in combination with, for instance, ibuprofen or heart medications.

The EPA has backed off fixing the legal meaning of "natural" for decades. It is close to being a meaningless term. It is also redundant; all whole leaf Artisan tea is naturally natural.

"Organic" is a certification process that is expensive, bureaucratic, often corrupt, and unaffordable and unneeded by many small growers who make superb teas that go beyond organic to comprehensive biodynamic management of every aspect of tea, terrain and environment.

Green tea does not appear to have different degrees of impact on any aspect of health than black teas. The differences in chemical composition are narrow and there's no tidy division between the teas. Green tea is softer and lighter which may make it more appealing as a semi-medication, based on "it goes down easily."

The claims made by most marketers of tea-as-health-diet-and-weight-shrinker are nonsense, misusing scientific terms and presenting strings of anecdotes as "proven" facts. Worse, many of the products they push are health dangers. Just about every industry, research and lifestyle study of tea extracts in capsule form rings alarm bells.

The scientific evidence is unchallengeable. Any impacts that tea has on any aspect of health or weight are at the very best possible but not proven and any claim otherwise is well-intentioned overenthusiastic exaggeration or irresponsible falsehood.

From a broader lifestyle perspective, tea does seem to play a useful but minor role in healthy living that contributes to but does not cause weight and health improvements. This is apparent in the many studies that focus on the diets and health regimes of people for whom weight, stress management and physical performance are matters of daily attention and even critical concern.

Well-studied examples are racehorse jockeys who must meet weight requirements on a daily basis and must lose pounds between waking and riding the same afternoon, endurance athletes, and accredited hospital diets for patients.

None of these includes tea in more than very small quantities that support the broader nutrition regime. In most instances, it is limited not encouraged, with water viewed as far more beneficial. Tea helps balance energization and calming. A little goes a long way. This is in direct contradiction of the tea-as-magic view, which makes assertive recommendations that more is better: 4-8 cups of green tea a day is not atypical. Effective practice focuses on less at the right time and in combination with the right foods.

This makes a lot of sense. If you look at tea as part of healthy living rather than a causal factor creating it, then it's easy to see how it helps. Here's the lifestyle profile:

Tea is an easy drink to incorporate into your routines. The

studies of jockeys see it as providing a slight boost to the system, stimulating the speeding up of fat-burning and calorie reduction. The small caffeine in one cup offsets the lethargy that is often a byproduct of a light diet. For British soldiers, it gave offered a far bolder boost made welcome in harsh conditions by the hotness of the tea. For dieters, it adds a safe and flavorful extra to the far more cleansing and filling hydration of water.

In general tea encourages or goes along with foods that are fresh, light, often sweet but also likely to be fresh vegetables, fruit and fish (sushi and sencha, for instance). It provides a little nutrition and stimulation of the digestive system from all the antioxidants, theanine, flavonols, etc. that it contains. Though none of these are proven in their impacts and benefits, the discouraging "may" and "further study is needed" of the scientific research can be more optimistically restated as "certainly don't hurt and probably help."

Caffeine: Stop worrying so much

No discussion of tea is complete without addressing caffeine. It's generally a primary factor in deciding whether to make it your main drink, substitute herbal teas (chamomile is the main soother of choice), or stick to low-caffeine greens and, more recently, "white" ones marketed as even lower than low.

Caffeine is largely seen as a "problem." The line of apologetic defense of tea is then along the lines of: "Yes, chugging ten energy drinks is not healthy... Caffeine's addictive and scary in its overdose effects... But, well, tea's not as bad as coffee... Green tea has less caffeine... OK, low caffeine tea in bags may taste dreadful and be bitter but it's good for you. And you can always try herbal teas..."

It makes sense to be more positive in viewing caffeine as a characteristic of tea rather than a negative danger alert: "Caffeine is good, not bad, for health for most people... Enjoy the tea you like – most of the green tea dogma is nonsense... If you switch to herbal teas, read the ingredients very, very carefully... And don't be fooled by the term "natural."

How much do you yourself worry about caffeine? Too much? Not enough? Not a concern? Here are some facts – not opinions – about it. Some of them may shift your answer.

The medically recommended safe limit for caffeine is 400 milligrams a day. The chart below shows the average caffeine levels for teas and alternative drinks.

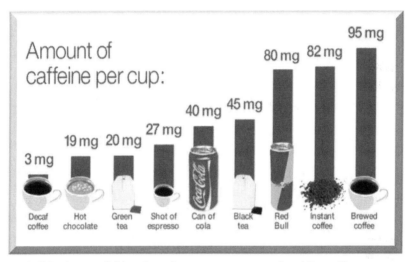

Caffeine is controllable: of equal concern are sugar and avoiding coffee excess.

These are just approximations. Drip coffee, for instance, is higher per milliliter than regular percolated coffee and espresso is much more caffeine-loaded. Black tea varies from around 20 milligrams when brewed for two minutes to 50 at five minutes. A white tea made from the finest buds has 75 mg. A white that contains more mature leaf and is less packed with the health-associated nutrients may be 25.

The message here is that there's nothing much to worry about. You can safely drink ten to twenty cups of tea of multiple colors before you hit the recommended daily limit. That's for anyone in sound health, without heart, hypertension or blood pressure problems, and not pregnant. For the smaller at risk fraction of the population, the obvious advice about *any* caffeinated drink is simple: Don't touch it.

Caffeine is a psychoactive drug with the same properties as heroin. They operate on areas of the brain and nervous system in the same way. Both are addictive and withdrawal symptoms are marked, though manageable for caffeine, with an extreme reaction of headaches and depression lasting 1-5 days. Message: Worry, or at least be careful.

But don't make it Social Enemy #1. Caffeine doesn't build up in the body and half of it disappears in about six hours. For a light caffeine tea containing 20 mg a cup, you won't really notice the effects and for a 40-mg tea drunk at, say, 8 a.m., half has gone from your body by 2 pm.

Change the am to pm, though, and you will still have some of the jolt effect at 2 am. Hence the tradition of black tea at breakfast and green for later in the day. Coffee is a different issue: the average 95 mg in just one cup is quite likely to have a nighttime impact.

The US is only middling in its per capita consumption. By far the highest level is in Scandinavian nations and well over twice that of the US. Their life expectancy ranks in the top ten globally, 2-3 years longer than the US average. Message: The general caffeine impact is overhyped. There is no reason to avoid tea just because of caffeine.

The broader issue is the pluses and minuses for yourself. Caffeine has many positives and is part of what makes tea flavorful. 80-90% of the population enjoys it as a mild stimulant that is quickly absorbed in the body. It has been reliably shown to improve short-term memory retention, something that students pulling an all-nighter to get ready for a mid-term know full well, without scientific evidence needed. One tea company pithily summarizes the upside as caffeine "clears the mind and elevates the spirit."

There are several alternative "teas" that are caffeine-free. Don't touch decaffeinated tea. It sounds like a good idea and the packaging will make it seem even better as "naturally decaffeinated." It isn't at all natural, but because the chemical solvent ethyl acetate used in the most common process is found in plants, the word can be legally used.

Obviously, your decision about caffeine is a personal choice that should take the facts and messages into consideration but not be driven by them. The core issue is: are you comfortable about making any caffeinated drink one that you consume several times a day? If not, don't drink tea. If so, drink the type you most like; from a health and safety perspective it doesn't make much difference whether it's a green, black or oolong.

As with so many aspects of the tea taste-health equation, you don't need to give up one to get the other. That a tea is low caffeine doesn't mean it's a good tea. Beware the "white" teas being marketed on that basis. That a full-tasting black tea is higher in caffeine doesn't make it unhealthier.

If you drink fewer than six cups a day, there is no reason to count caffeine milligrams anyway. The historical pattern of tea drinking makes plenty of sense: a morning wake up black tea and lighter oolong, green or top rate white for the late afternoon. Caffeine in teas gets more attention than it really merits.

Tea: pesticides and contamination

Pesticides, pollution and environmental damage must be at the very least a background concern for tea drinkers: What do you need to know to make sure that you don't buy something that puts your health at risk?

No one can provide definitive answers. This is an area where just about any opinion can be found, from scare stories to shrug it all off, and there's an information overload that is close to impossible to sort out. The evidence suggests that tea is safer than most agricultural products and that you can minimize your own health risks by focusing your choices on mountain-grown teas.

There are three main areas of concern about pesticides and the more general risks from environmental damage: (1) the health reflex, (2) the China association, and (3) tabloid science.

When you add all this up, what can you reliably conclude? Should you be fearful, cautious, indifferent or comfortable? Here's just one tea drinker's assessment, based on a fairly exhaustive tracking of news, scientific reports, tea industry position statements, blogs and government and regulatory announcements:

Be wary of broad scare stories and shrug-it-all-off ones that rely on science but do not provide research details or evidentiary support. When you read a striking short piece that provides assertive claims and figures, you just can't tell how reliable it is.

While there is no reason to assume the major tea firms are pure of motive and not using every chemical resource at their command, many of the attacks on them don't quite ring true. There are too many claims and not enough replication of isolated results. The tea giants are highly skilled in process management, quality control, sourcing and blending. It doesn't seem in their interests to flout the fairly strict rules for tea imports. Most of them make certifications of quality and purity part of their branding: the Ethical Tea Alliance, UDA organic, etc.

Buy single estate and pedigree teas from mountain regions. Today's best tea still comes from the places that dominate its historical reputation and craft. Some smallholders teas the edges of law and make some use of chemicals. In some instances they have limited choices: monoculture, adaptation of insects to standard chemical sprays and shifting climatic patterns are a threat they can't ignore.

Avoid generic blends, low end tea bags, anonymous teas from unspecified sources, and lowland mass farming commodity tea. This is not a matter of snobbery and many of these meet the core standards of agricultural quality and safety, but there are just too many gaps in the supply, distribution, and production systems to be sure.

Volume production of cheap food inevitably means pesticides. The humid subtropical climates in which tea grows are nurseries for lots and lots of insects and critters. The estimated crop loss from uncontrolled farming is anywhere from 10% to 55%.

"Pesticide" is too often translated as "poisonous" and at best a necessary evil. But most pesticides are completely safe and there are others that in trace amounts pose no health risks. Many are short-lived and while around 85% are synthetic, there is an increasing adoption of natural ones as part of biodynamic farming.

As with antibiotics used in everyday medical treatment, there are broad spectrum pesticides that zap everything and ones that are more targeted. Overuse of pesticides, as with antibiotics, can weaken their effectiveness and be literally overkill. One of the problems in moving to natural pesticides is that they take much longer than synthetic ones to take effect, 6-9 months versus weeks or even days. The worry is that many giant farms and smallholders that produce low grade tea have underinvested in bush and soil renewal and must rely on chemical boosts.

All their incentives are to cut costs now – and not invest in future quality and environmental sustainability. Smallholders face growing and very, very severe poverty as prices continue to erode. In many countries, they are threatened by takeover of their land, and they are naturally ready to use anything that helps their marginal business, including using banned and bootleg pesticides, some of which are associated with neurological damage.

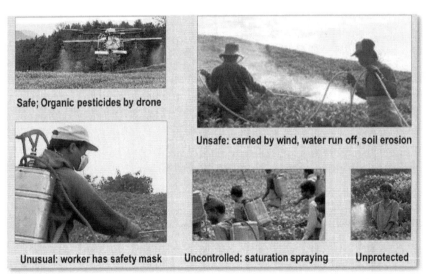

This is the norm in Agribusiness farming. It very much applies to tea bags.

The problems are most acute in markets where consumption is mostly domestic. By and large – somewhat weaselly words for "we think but can't be sure" – tea imports seem to be at least as safe as fruits and meats. Reliance on exports requires meeting the standards of the import monitoring agencies of the EU, Japan and a few other nations that have tightened regulation and increased sanctions. One of the main reasons to doubt the most extreme scare stories is that there is growing sophistication and security in handling tea imports, partly because tea is such an integral element of everyday life in so many countries.

The Artisan tradition is responding by strengthening its biodynamic methods, streamlining supply chains, and becoming very selective in its use of pesticides and fertilizers. Japan and Germany have rejected imports from several countries, forcing them to upgrade their growers' practices.

Agribusiness mass production of low end teas is much more "iffy." The major brands seem to be both responsible and efficient in managing their own operations and in buying leaf. There doesn't appear to be much substance in the accusations that their teas are packed with residues from pesticides.

The China association

"Tea-n-China" is another verbal elision, like tea-n-health. It's natural to associate "tea" with China, even though half of US tea imports are from Argentine and about 30% more from African growers. China does not exactly have a sterling reputation for food safety. Scandal is the more general label: corruption, contamination, pollution of air, soil and water, and fraud.

Published interviews with many Western tea experts suggest that this Chinese stereotype is incomplete. They point to reasonably effective government tightening of loopholes and aggressive increase in sanctions aimed at protecting China's export markets, though some doubt these will be much more than window-dressing.

They are generally much more positive about the pedigree mountain teas. Even close to the massively polluted cities and manufacturing regions, the mountain winds and seasonal shifts keep the hills swept clean. The elite tea growing communities are moving firmly to protect their heritage.

Key regions like Wuyi, noted for its rock oolongs, have improved waste management and burning of trash. The Longjing growers of Dragonwell, routinely identified as China's best tea, are collaborating to protect water supply and quality. Before a tea can be sold in Guangzhou's famous market of 3,000 shops it must be taste-tested in a lab, which also offers free services for growers to send their samples.

The contamination problems seem less ones of nation as type of terrain. There are three major sources of agricultural harm: heavy metals in the soil, water contamination and pesticides. The metals are a roadside problem, from passing cars. The mountains are not auto-friendly and lack roads and traffic. This discourages heavy use of pesticides simply because it is too expensive to lug the stuff up there.

The climate is also less the playground of bugs and pests than the more humid lowlands. So far, acid rain and the appalling smokestack airborne pollution that is at crisis levels in the big cities of China and India doesn't seem to have affected mountain plants but the chain effects of carbon monoxide are uncertain and likely to be pervasive.

Even Darjeeling now has a traffic pollution problem. The tea fields of Assam are often next to oil drilling operations. Korean and Japanese land prices are shrinking the areas available for tea growing and housing and business complexes are encroaching on what was only a few years well-protected, pristine and packed with now disappearing biodiversity. Fertilizers and run offs are lowering water quality.

China is not the main problem for the future of tea. It's a broader ecological issue.

Tabloid science

Would you like a scary Frankencrop alarm analysis of tea? Take your pick... One that created headlines and has been widely quoted is a report by Greenpeace that "More than half of Chinese tea is tainted with banned pesticides." Eighteen medium-grade teas from leading companies were tested by "an accredited third-party laboratory." It found that every single sample contained three or more pesticides, including at least one that is banned from use. Almost 10% of workers using pesticide applicators suffered pesticide poisoning.

This is striking and disconcerting. Is it true? You just can't tell. The companies totally deny the validity of the tests and point to the refusal to publish the data or source; the results haven't been replicated and the teas all meet strict import standards.

Another Greenpeace study states that 60% of Indian tea samples contain pesticide residues above the maximum permitted by the European Union. The Chairman of the India Tea Board dismisses this as "completely baseless." A famous or infamous US report that names many top brands as pesticide-packed turns out to have been sponsored by an investment firm short-selling – betting on a drop in stock price of one of the companies. But the lab analysis has been accepted by some experts as reliable. Again, how can you tell?

Because the science of tea is so complex, the analysis of pesticides gets reported in broad headlines of X% of teas or more than Y% above MRL (maximal residual level) but the base research is at a molecular scale.

Much of the work now includes developing precise measurement tools such as gas chromatography, immunoassay and atomic absorption methods. Here's a random extract from a study: "... using hyphenation of SPME in a head-space mode with a comprehensive two-dimensional GC coupled with high-speed time-of-flight MS..."

This doesn't translate easily to even the best of journalism, where headlines need to be big, messages definite and figures understandable. The presentation and interpretation gap is illustrated in reports on a big scare in Japan that has led to the government banning sales from several major tea growing regions.

This was a response to the high levels of cesium radiation in tea leaves that is a direct outcome of the nuclear power plant meltdown in 2011. Domestic and foreign demand plummeted. As one farmer comments "When people are fearful, they are not going to buy your products, no matter how many times they tell you they are safe."

The farmers are telling them exactly that; the government regulations measure the concentration in the dried leaves, not the final tea product. You would have to drink two hundred bottles of green tea every day for a year before there would be any health risk. But the simple tabloid headline blocks the scientific exegesis.

Just about all the reporting on the scientific studies of tea is suspect. It naturally tends to the scare end of the alarm/don't worry spectrum. Headlines are not enough. That is not to discount the scare stories; they may lack needed detail but can be useful alerts. But the Greenpeace studies just don't pass the core tests of scientific research; no respected journal would accept them for publication. The issues of pollution, contamination ad safety rest on the details of science. Tabloids obscure those details.

Tea and weight loss: lessons from jockeys, athletes

The question is simple: Does drinking green tea directly create weight loss? The scientific answer is simple, too: No. There is no scientific evidence whatsoever, only hopeful hints. The medical answer is also a No, plus be careful – very careful – about what the "green tea" is and does to you. Green tea extract supplements (GTE), one of the aggressively marketed weight loss products, are listed as a significant health risk, not aid. They are highly concentrated with dosage levels 10 times the safe recommendations in many instances. It's ironic – and toxic – that the aid touted for its anti-oxidant benefits becomes a pro-oxidant that attacks healthy cells, with many reported deaths from liver damage.

The counter view is that green tea is proven as a diet aid (sellers: "*9 Stunning Herbal Weight Loss Teas*", "*20 Teas That Melt Belly Fat*"), core to healthy living (lifestyle advocates: "*The Green Tea Lifestyle*", "*Winter Wellness with Green Tea*") and a media magic potion hype ("*Miracle Weight Loss Teas.*")

It's a somewhat pointless debate. Here's a more useful perspective. Shift the focus from the tea-weight loss link to the reverse. What lessons can we learn from the experience of people whose very livelihood depends on keeping their weight down, often at the daily level, while remaining strong and fit? Where does tea fit into their dietary regimes?

The picture that emerges from the wide literature on how jockeys, dancers, and athletes handle the challenge is consistent. These are STFs – Stay Thin Folks.

Tea is very much a design element for helping them get a breakfast start-off that combines good nutritional balance, an energy boost and a relaxed sense of mind. It is not seen as a factor that in any way directly causes weight loss. There is not one study that recommends even two cups at a time or multiple cups a day.

A common theme is that tea stimulates the body's mechanisms to start burning up some calories. Again, correlation not causation; the simple reality is that weight loss is a function of calories taken in minus calories out.

It does not recommend herbal teas or GTEs (green tea extracts). This is in direct contrast to many of the tea weight loss promises, which too often are little more than crash diets, and most of which are not in fact tea but herbal mixes. There is one called ballerina's tea that real dancers are warned against. It's a straight laxative purge and "colon roto-rooter." It's *not* tea. Tea always contains a small amount of caffeine.

A typical alert from the American Heart Association (2016) warns that natural cold remedies, supplements, herbal compounds and green tea pose a danger to heart patients, including weakening their heart muscles and increasing sodium and fluid retention. The interaction of herbal brews and medications is a regular topic: ibuprofen, valerian and even chamomile pose hidden risks that fall outside the FDA's regulatory oversight.

Caffeine is a positive, not a negative. Caffeinated tea raises metabolic rate: "you turn on the fat-burning spigot a little bit more." Most of the miracle products are herbs, undermining the very basis of the tea-weight loss link. Water is far more important than tea in ensuring constant rehydration through the day, in small and frequent. Sip, rather than gulp, your way to a lesser you. Green tea is preferred mainly for being pleasant and smooth to sip, but black tea, sugar and milk are often recommended – in small amounts of one cup – to balance energy and relaxation.

An intriguing result in a few studies is that tea seems to help in dealing with a problem reported by jockeys; a slight depression and aggression that seems to reflect the body/mind's reaction against strict and non-enjoyable diet constraints. Dietary changes often have negative downer effects on mood.

All this is very consistent with the inconclusive nature of almost all the scientific research. Where there is some evidence of a link between tea and weight loss, it's impossible to sort out exactly much how the tea is the explanation, versus the associated shift in breakfast (very much the focus of the STF studies), or even addition of a beer for evening relaxation and sugar fix (again, a common STF tip).

A major implication for people in their everyday life is that while the scientific evidence does not support claims about its direct impacts on weight, in its basic form with no additives, "natural" flavors or herbal ingredients, it has no apparent negative side effects. It is by far the best beverage choice for weight management compared with colas with sugar, high caffeine coffee, lead-laden iced tea and bottled drinks, and of course alcohol.

The claims beyond this have no validity in either science, medicine or STF practice. Here's one of the standard garbage media pitches that the green tea weight loss hype leads to, from Redbook magazine in December, 2015, *Mom Lost 100 Pounds in One Year Drinking Weight Loss Tea.*

The lady is 5'1"" and weighed 210lbs at 18. "" Feeling miserable about my way I looked only made me want to eat more." As a result of her unhappiness, she developed "bad eating habits: two pieces of buttered toast for breakfast, two chocolate bars for a snack, two grilled cheese sandwiches with chips for lunch, greasy pizza for dinner, and drink either sugary soda or five cups of tea with milk and sugar nearly every day. "I'd always dunk a couple of cookies in them too."

"People told me green tea was a 'superfood'" so she gave it a try – nine cups a day of green tea. She hated the bitter taste and had to force herself to drink it. She has lost 100 lbs.

Maybe reducing her calorie intake had a little to do with this. So, too, did the hourly tea routine in shaping her day and keeping her hydrated. The volume of liquid in itself reduces appetite. Nine cups of tea, however, adds known health risks of its own.

Her summary is one that nutritionists readily agree with: "For me, it [green tea] is not a fad. It's a lifestyle."

Sweet Dreams: drinking tea at bedtime

It's ironic that enthusiasts for tea as a wonderful aid to good physical health so often at the same time ring the alarm bells about its dangers after 6 pm. The calming, soothing enhancer of psychological well-being turns into *"No caffeine just before bedtime"* as almost a diktat. Tea will keep you awake, disrupt your sleep patterns, and create a "sleep deficit" that will push you to consuming more tea (or the demon coffee) next day.

Sleep used to be a simple process of snuggle down in your bed at the end of day. It is now a real challenge for many people: disruptive work schedules, time zone shifts, early morning gearing up for the highway commute battles, and late nights – you know them well. Caffeine has become embedded in our routines in dealing with many of these.

But what about bedtime? What drink can *you* personally choose that will help you get to sleep, stay asleep and wake up feeling fresh? Must you avoid caffeine entirely, hold it to a low amount or pick only certain types of tea? You have three main choices, each of which comes with general positives and negatives but also affects individuals in entirely different ways:

Coffee: High caffeine; energizing, not relaxing. Many coffee drinking cultures such as France, Scandinavia and Mexico, aren't concerned with caffeine as a problem, but there is no question that it does have a direct and disruptive effect on sleep for many individuals.

Tea: Often assumed to be in the problem category in terms of caffeine, misleadingly so. Offers a wide variety of choices that many tea drinkers are scared away from taking up only because of clichés about caffeine and arrant nonsense about green and white teas versus black and oolong ones. May be an option to forego for the caffeine-intolerant, but not an inevitable cause of sleep disruption for most.

Herbal drinks: Not the preferred and healthy choice that they are too often touted as. Many side effects, some quite dangerous.

Sodas, alcohol and just plain water are also options, of course, but these three are the ones most likely to be part of you being able to nod off rather than grimace in response to "Sleep well."

The central issue in picking among them is caffeine, of course. The commonsense view is that caffeine is a stimulant that you should avoid entirely around bedtime. "Caffeine-intolerance" is very real for many people and levels of caffeine in your bedtime drink often do have a dramatic impact on sleep.

But caffeine-as-villain is too narrow a perspective. It is analogous to a major Swedish study of work that aimed at identifying differences in stress among professions and specific activities. Subjects wore body monitors that tracked their blood pressures, heart beats, perspiration and galvanic responses throughout the day.

The project was abandoned after a few months. The data showed that nothing in their work had even a fraction of the stress created by driving to it. Similarly, the contributions of tea, coffee or herbal brews to quality of sleep are dwarfed by the wider dynamics of your routines and physical makeup. (There's evidence that some types of caffeine-intolerance may be caused by genetic variations of the Adenosine A_{2A} receptor gene, in which case, you don't have any real choices.)

Here's an impressionistic summary of the scientific research studies on caffeine and sleep. It is very muddly and doesn't add up to a clear picture of the landscape. One study, for example, looks definitive. It shows that caffeine reduced average sleeping time among its subjects by two hours a night, increased the number of awakenings, and doubled the time of wakefulness.

However...

The caffeine was set at 300 milligrams, to equal the average daily intake, but here delivered in one dissolved dose. There were just six subjects, all middle-aged. The caffeine is the equivalent of 8-12 cups of whole leaf tea at a single sitting. Contextual issues applicable to real tea in a real setting such as the heat of the tea, how long it took to cool and drink, the range of subjects' ages, and bladder management are entirely absent. All the study really says is that a huge dose of coffee or tea is guaranteed to have an effect.

This pattern comes up again and again in studies. The caffeine is generally a tea extract, pill or powder. This omits other elements of the leaf's chemistry. For instance, L-theanine compounds seem to have a relaxing impact on the brain. They offset some of the energizing impacts of caffeine. But they are not included in the study by letting the whole leaf compounds interact. It's all just caffeine not tea.

And an absurd amount of just caffeine. Most studies treat subjects with a 250-400 mg hit. Of course, that extreme input will create extreme outputs. If you make yourself a single cup of whole leaf tea, it will typically contain just 20-40 mg. Studies that use doses of 40 to 80 do show some largely small but consistent sleep disruptions.

Many of these are dependent on levels and times of caffeine consumption during the day, with different effects on morning sleepiness, cognitive performance and even finger muscle strengths (500 mg of caffeine doubles it – 12 or more cups of tea; now why does that not seem surprising?) One study concludes that anyone who consumes 500-600 mg of caffeine a day "is likely" to have sleep difficulties. Anyone who does that has more to worry about than taking a nap.

Large-scale repeated samples and longitudinal analyses show that anxiety, mood and overall body comfort account for most of sleep disruptions, more than health status. Financial stress is one of the most cited factors. Forces that help build these improve sleep.

Poverty is not a controllable factor, alas, but ones that are include lowering the bedroom temperature, (research shows a consistent positive relationship between sound sleep and below average heat), selection of music at night, and breathing exercises.

The role of your bedtime drink then expands from caffeine-sensitivity to mood and comfort "management." It's worth noting that the daytime value of tea has for millennia been seen as its calming and encouragement of meditation, mainly through its rituals and ceremonies. This has been the core of Buddhist tea practice, the Japanese tea ceremony, and the British "let's all sit down and have a nice cup of tea."

Can tea help you get in the mood to sleep? This doesn't have to involve more than brewing a special tea in your favorite pot and just taking time out. Exactly what tea or which alternative drink you choose should fit into this context.

Pick any of them. If you are drinking just one nighttime cup, then 60 grams of caffeine, the upper end of the white-green-oolong-black scale, will not have a substantial direct disruptive effect and in any case, that is small compared to the mood/comfort contribution. For most people, black tea will be a little too brisk and sharpen their senses rather than help them drift into sleepiness. Green teas offer a wide range of flavor, with slightly vegetal ones that are crisp but can be a little too drying, and sweeter and floral brews that are gentle and very satisfying. Some of those will be higher in caffeine – Japanese Sencha for example – but just right for mood: soft and relaxing.

Now for the tough option... Herbal teas. These can be dangerous choices. They are advertised for their Sleepy-something value and for being caffeine-free and natural. Most are processed for packaging in tea bags. Many meet their promise; they are soothing and aromatic, warming and easy to digest. Their selling messages often rest on the contrast of caffeine-bad/herbal-good distinction.

There's a lot of herbal bad, though. The very fact that chamomile, valerian, lavender, lemongrass, spearmint and other common ingredients in them have proven health benefits in and of itself is a warning. It means that they interact with the body at the neurological and chemical level; they are not inert. Remember that Lucretia Borgia's reputation as a poisoner (more a libel than a likely truth) rested on her herb-gathering and blending skills; her sleepytime brew was for ever.

Many of the ingredients mentioned earlier are powerful. Chamomile has been used since the dynasties of Ancient Egypt for its easing of digestion, antibacterial properties and soothing depressive impacts. Those come with risks of bleeding, severe drowsiness if mixed with alcohol, and significant dangers in pregnancy. Spearmint is healthy but easily affects kidney functions when mixed with a variety of other medications.

Valerian is a marvelous sedative and sleep aid but physicians routinely warn of its many dangers and strongly urge getting specific advice, avoiding its use in conjunction with many medical prescriptions, discontinuing long-term use, and stopping any consumption for two weeks before any surgical treatment. It acts very much like a medical anesthetic.

This statement is commonplace in reviews of valerian: "However, [this and several other herbs] are powerful drugs that should be used only under the consultation of a medical professional, not used casually as a beverage."

Which of these herbal teas is safe (1) by itself, (b) in combinations, (3) with over the counter pills, (d) with your prescribed medication? How do you know?

The trade-offs are compounded by the fact that none of the main herbal sleep aids has been proven to have any measurable effect. The main word summarizing results of research studies is "inconclusive." But, coming back to the value of a beverage at night in providing warm hydration, a relaxing mood-builder and a pleasant taste, if it works for you, that's fine. Maybe your reaction is "subjective" but getting to sleep can be as much a matter of mind as body.

Here are some recommendations if you are a regular tea drinker in this neutral range of caffeine concerns:

Recognize that bedtime tea doesn't have to mean herbal tea. If you like it, choose it. But do, please, learn a little about what's in it. Do not assume it is always beneficial.

Test drive your teacup. Try drinking a whole leaf caffeinated tea that really fits your mood requirements and see how that works out over, say, a week. Obviously, if the caffeine does affect you, change gears.

In many instances, for instance, when you last drank tea can have a spillover impact on the rhythms of your mind and body. You may want to drink your bedtime tea at bedtime, with the risk that the caffeine will be more active during your first phase of sleep. Or you may decide to take it several hours earlier so that it will have worked much of its way through your system well before dawn's early hints.

Without getting gimmicky and dressing yourself up in Japanese tea ceremony rig, match your tea to your relaxation routine. Tea and reading naturally go together in this regard: to curl up with a good book implies with a good tea.

Don't expect tea, coffee, cognac, herbal brews, or green tea supplement pills to "make" you sleep. They may help but there is no evidence that they have more than a marginal value.

Finally, here are some teas from the *Tea Tips* portfolio to consider that offer a fine combination of sleep help:

White: Silver Needle: expensive but affordable for one cup a day. Choose the best: China Yunnan, Darjeeling estate names, Sri Lanka.

Japan green: Gyokuro (Japanese): Very expensive and for occasional drinking. Also high caffeine. But exquisite and a sensory delight – light and rich. Sencha: pick a good grade. Recommendation is Kagoshima or Uji: very little astringency and not too light. Houjicha: smoky and leaves a pleasant goodnight aftertaste. Kukicha twig tea, smooth, soft, leaves a mellow taste in your mouth.

China green: Jasmine Pearl for its smoothness, absence of astringency and floral freshness. Yunnan Mao Feng for its buttery feel and refreshing light taste.

Oolong: Taiwan Tung Ting. Fuller than greens and whites but not too much so for bedtime. Adds a smoky flavor that lingers pleasantly.

Black: Don't be afraid to try a China Keemun or a lighter Indian Darjeeling. Play around with the brewing time to lower the astringency.

Tea is such a pleasure throughout the day. There is no dogmatic reason not to keep it so at night. Yes, caffeine may impose a block on you but that is not a given. Think of tea as part of designing your bedtime mood and routine. Pick your drink on that basis. Your body will let you know if you've got it right.

Buying tea

The expanding choice space

When you shop around for tea, there are four distinct places to look, shown as circles below: (1) supermarkets and groceries; (2) local tea and gourmet stores, (3) Web site sellers, and (4) luxury providers.

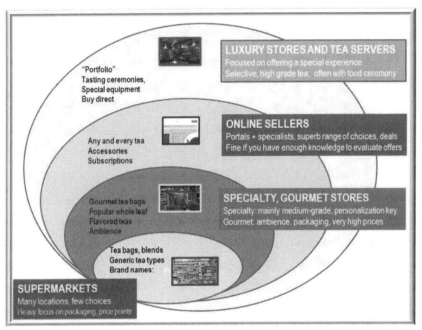

The shopping choices expand as the locations narrow in number.

Where to buy can be as important for tea shopping as what. Apart from obvious issues of price, service and stocks, there are more subtle ones relating to quality, supply chain, and warranty. A distinct problem with tea is assessing how good or even exactly what it is from either the package, looking at and smelling the tea, or reading the sales ad, especially when that's pitched around claims about health, weight loss, detox, etc.

Rather than point you to specific sellers, *Tea* Tips steers you towards the best places to look and the pluses and minuses of each type of seller. The logic is to be a guide not a reviewer. Here's the general advice:

Supermarkets and grocery stores: Don't bother if it offers just shelves of packages and the odd tin. A few will have a fine tea section; check it out by comparing its cheese selection to get an idea of quality, freshness, and assistants' knowledge. If those look good, the teas are also likely to be worth buying since they show the store can manage perishable, specialty goods that require skill in sourcing and quality control.

The teas are generally supplied by wholesalers and you are unlikely to find anything unusual. But quite often there are interesting Assams, Wuyi oolongs and blends.

Local specialty teas shops and tea houses: Take them for what they are and don't expect too much. A first-rate specialty store is a joy and usually has an opinionated owner/manager with both knowledge, access to local sources in China, India and Japan, and enthusiasm.

Those which offer table service for teas provide the opportunity for you to try something selected to stand out as Very Different and for the owner to carry a wider inventory. It may be hard for a small operation to sell a pound of a honey orchid Dan Cong oolong at around $100 – 200 cups – but easy to serve just 50 cups at, say, $3. And for you to try a new tea that may have you buying two ounces at checkout.

Mall and boutique gourmet stores: Oh dear. Too many of these offer ambience, great visual displays and layouts, wonderful packaging and tea that is not very good. It is generally at least twice the price of specialty shops and online sellers.

Their marketing focuses on the snobbish side of tea with the intimation that they bring special expertise in locating, selecting and blending their teas. In practice, they rely on wholesalers – "Packed for Us in New Orleans" – and blends that have a strong aroma that has an immediate appeal when you smell it in the store.

The simplest way to check out one of these stores is to look at the price for a few select teas. If they average more than $6 an ounce, you are in the specialty class and this should be a pedigree tea. $12 for a mall oolong is not in that class, nor is $20 for a fruit tea sampler. Yes, that floral blend smells appealing; the better upmarket grocery stores have ones as good at half the price.

The best deals in these upmarket elegant stores are upmarket elegant accessories. These are easier to source, don't pose problems of freshness and storage, and often are state-of-the-market designs.

Online portals: There are two types of online sellers: the malls – portals – where you park and either browse around or go direct to one of the stores, and the many individualized ones that you access directly by name.

Amazon and eBay are the two major portals that offer many teas and tea stores. If you know what you are looking for and have a fair knowledge of teas, you can find excellent deals, but equally there are many very dubious offers.

Some of the best sites within the portals are Chinese sellers, who use them as their distribution base. The quality of service, packing and shipping now matches that of US suppliers. It's also worth checking if you get a better deal from the well-established online sellers on their own sites or a portal.

A key in portal shopping is the adage of if the deal seems too good to be true, however tempting it is, skip it. It's tempting to scan by price first, then the tea. Always look at the leaf before the price.

Online specialty sellers: This is a rich and expanding space of choice. Just about any fine tea can be found on offer from a few established Web brands, a range of reliable sites that have a well-focused range of well-described teas, and a bigger variety of stores that have some distinctive style and inventory.

Some of these are very pricy. Others will offer, say, a good choice of oolongs, but only a few will list ones they have sourced directly from individual growers, or present ten different senchas, each with some small feature of region, season, processing style, leaf characteristics, aging, etc.

It's difficult to offer general shopping tips here. Finding the stores is very much a matter of serendipity. Where possible, it makes best sense to try out the site with a test purchase of a few small amounts, preferably two ounces if available, and expand your exploration.

In addition, while the portals are most useful for broad exploration, with the specialty sellers shop into their areas of strength. For example, there are outstanding Indian sellers who don't cover Japanese and Chinese teas and vice versa. Nor should they. Indeed, it's difficult to envision a provider that can do justice to a broad range of Darjeelings plus Assam blacks as well as Chinese plus Taiwanese oolongs and also Japanese sencha, matcha and gyokuro.

Luxury providers: These are downtown big city special attractions and more for the tourist experience than for value. They include a few elite stores that sell only scarce and highest grade teas, the five-star hotel offering an afternoon tea gala with reverent service, sarnies – whoops, sorry, cucumber sandwiches – and a menu of teas for all tastes. You get the silver pots and accoutrements. Finally, there are tea houses that combine a sense of history with excellent teas.

They're OK and several of those in cities like Paris, Tokyo, Hong Kong and Dubai do provide a great show. If you are more interested in the tea, though, you can do as well buying two ounces of an outstanding tea that is way above your daily routine and price and making it at home, where you can have complete control of the brewing process.

It's surprising and bothersome how many of the palaces have too long a distance between where the hot water source and your table plus too many minutes before the server reaches it. The water is not quite right. It should be for $30.

Obviously, you will have your own preferences and habits in shopping. The *Tea Tips* suggestion is for teas is not to let this get you stuck with the familiar. Many tea drinkers don't know that there are choices beyond the limits of their current habitual purchases. It's natural to stick with a brand name in the supermarket, a safe sounding loose leaf tea at a reasonable price in a tea store, a designer tin with a Name, or a popular and high-rated option online (including Amazon).

Unfortunately, the safe choices are largely bland and uninteresting ones. Applying rules of thumb based on the tried and true of experience and brand awareness will lock you in to second- or even third-rate tea bags and blends (supermarket), medium grades of high volume wholesaler and packager whole leaf (the average tea store), and online deals that are a little hit or miss – that's where there are top rate choices but also many "too good to be true" bargains that are marketing myth.

A major goal of *Tea Tips* is to help you find the good and true ones. Keep in mind four questions; if you're not comfortable in the answers, shop elsewhere:

Do I know what I'm looking for in terms of specific teas, type or taste or do I want to find something really different? What's this store/site offer in this regard?

What information does it provide on the *ingredients* of the teas? Country, region, harvest, blend, grade?

Is it mainly selling the package or the tea?

Do the staff know anything about tea or is this just another inventory stock item?

Here's what you can expect from each circle in the diagram of the choice space.

Supermarkets and grocery chains

This is the standard supermarket set of shelves. It looks better than it is, in terms of choice, price and quality.

Many different colors and packages, but very few differences in the teas

The teas on offer in the typical supermarket exclude the unusual and unfamiliar. There may be the occasional puehr in leaf, not brick, form or China oolong and plenty of blends but these are generic broken leaf and mass farmed. Japanese teas of any type or grade are not at all common in groceries. You are as likely to find a puehr bing as you are to fins a polar bear in the fish section. If you want to be a little adventurous and explore new teas, the supermarket shelf is about the last place to look. Don't bother.

The main products are brand name tea bags and blends plus private label low price bags. The larger and more upmarket ones offer plenty of flavored and herbal teas, some of which are of a decidedly higher standard than the breakfast teas competing in a crowded product space.

The supermarket selling points are packaging and "price point": clusters of bulk boxes of cheap bags in the $2-3 range, bags and tins of blends for $3-6, and flavored specialty teas in purchase units of $9-12, mostly bags. The teas will not be fresh; if they show expiration dates at all, they will be as long as 18 months in the future.

There may be house brands for most of the basic tea types, with labels that exploit the lack of international standardization of names, descriptions, countries of origin and quantity of leaf. Some of the more upmarket stores have a tea section. These are generally quite good. They are mainly stocked by large wholesalers who buy in bulk and sell in smaller units. Ones on self-service shelves tend to lose freshness because the tins are opened too many times and not protected from the air.

There's so much that you won't find, mainly because of the economics of the global industry. The profits in tea come from what is termed "downstream" in the supply chain: packaging, marketing and distribution, not the upstream growing and processing. This is the driving force along the Agribusiness path. The major international players are very skilled in getting the product to the consumer. To do this, they naturally simplify the upstream steps, starting with sourcing the leaf.

This won't change. The major brand names face an easily overlooked constraint on "premiumization" of the teas they sell: their supply chains are driven by volume, with little room for variety. Fine tea growing is the reverse: variety with little opportunity for volume.

There are over 37,000 supermarkets in the US and around the same in the UK, Germany and Japan. If a global tea brand wanted to launch, say, a new line of good whole leaf black teas in just 5,000 of these 80,000 or so stores and sell 50 four-ounce tins a week in each, that adds up to a total of around 1,500 metric tonnes of tea.

Maybe, they could begin with a good Nepalese tea, from the Ilam region. That's becoming very popular, is price-competitive and there are over 5,000 growers. But they produce just 1,600 metric tonnes of Orthodox Artisan leaf. Buying up the entire harvests would be needed to stock just a tiny fraction of a brand's retail outlets. As for a good Darjeeling, such as Margaret's Hope, the annual production is 250 tonnes, enough to stock the supermarkets with a tin a day.

So, forget the Margaret's Hope. There are 10,000 Nepal gardens and small farms producing CTC tea amounting to 16,000 tonnes. If the company could make it a Nepal blend.... Maybe, mix in some CTC from Bangladesh and Pakistan.... A little Malawi leaf could add color to the liquor. It wouldn't have to use the top leaf grades (TGFOP = "tippy" "golden" and "flowery") but can rely on much cheaper OP (basic) and BOP (broken leaf). Now, the seller has the volume but has eroded the quality. The tea can still be called a Nepal blend.

This line of analysis explains why you won't see a higher-grade Nepal tea, a single estate Darjeeling, one of the many well-priced and flavorful regional Ceylons, a pedigree oolong, a first-rate Yunnan green or a higher quality Japanese sencha. *What appears on the supermarket shelf is a function of the supply chain not the growers.* The tail wags the dog. This makes business sense and optimizes processes and capabilities, but it doesn't guide you to the best tea available and affordable.

Most casual tea drinkers are satisfied with the supermarket offers. They have the advantage of name recognition, which is why packaging is such a primary consideration for the brands. You pretty much know what you are getting. The purchase price is small, even if you are overpaying in comparison with a specialty whole leaf alternative. Once you find a tea you like, you can stay with it and be sure of finding it in most supermarkets and groceries.

But this is largely mediocre and it's not improving. Just as most people eat processed cheese for convenience and buy hot dogs and bologna on a routine grab-and-go basis, these are teas for drinking, not savoring – good enough and cheap enough.

Local specialty stores

Local tea stores with a broader inventory are scattered and harder to find. Their quality largely rests on the personality and knowledge of the owner. Many are optimistic ventures that run up against the commonplace barriers that limit – or sink – so many small businesses. To cover their fixed costs and low volume, they need to charge high markups.

Their generic problem is the size of a sale. They need at least $30 per purchase from foot traffic to cover their fixed costs. The breakeven gross margin on sales is around 150%; online stores can operate at much lower price markups though that is offset by the cost of free or reduced shipping. At $300,000 total revenues, they can be very profitable, but many are marginal and don't last long. They are very much like bookstores in the years before the Amazon and e-book digital transformation of buyer, product and seller.

Personality matters because the main value that store shopping adds over online ordering – as with the surviving successful bookstores – is advice, the ability to sample teas and a listener who can take your vague interests – "I don't really enjoy strong teas but I do enjoy XYZ English Breakfast" or "What are oolongs like?" — and point you to something special. Most of the store staff will be young and unlikely to be tea drinkers. They typically won't have a knowledge edge; the owner should.

The main differences among the specialty stores are inventory, both what they stock and where they get it. Some are owned by very knowledgeable people with good contacts. They draw on a network of tea buyers who can provide them with individualized items and in many instances, go direct to growers and their agents. Most, though, rely on wholesalers who offer them a standard range of teas, many of which will be bulk blends. What looks selective can be average and basic.

One way of getting a sense of this is to ask about teas that are just a little unusual. Check out if they are worth spending time browsing in by simply by picking a few of the megamountain brands described earlier: Alishan, Wuyi, Huangshan, Darjeeling, Uva, Nuwara Eliya, Xishuangbana, Uji, or Yunnan. You can't expect a store to carry these but one that doesn't have any of them is all normal but not special.

When you go into a tea store, there's one simple signal to look for. If you see lots of attractive teas out in the open on dishes or in large glass containers, exit. One of the critical factors in making sure that your good tea makes a good cup is storage. Tea has a Dracula complex: exposure to light kills it. It must be hidden from air, moisture and odors; tea absorbs these quickly, which is why it blends fruits and floral flavors into it so well. A basic feature of a good tea store is thus the tins. They should be kept closed and tightly sealed. The server will be careful and quick in opening and shutting them.

A second feature will be the labeling. They should be informative and describe the key elements of the tea: pedigree name and source. The minimum is something like: Darjeeling: first flush, single estate or China Yunnan Silver Tip Mao Feng. These are industry names that tell you just what you need to get a sense of the quality of the tea. When they are substituted with flashy marketing names you can assume that this is not a serious store.

Some of the traditional names of Chinese teas are very poetic – Precious Eyebrow, Iron Goddess of Mercy and Buddha's Palm – but you can look these up on your smartphone. But treat the pseudo-brand names as meaning just "a blend of teas from a packager or importer in New Orleans or on the West Coast." The pseudo- includes Jane Austen whatever, Masterpiece TV Series something and Tropical Floral Breeze salad. Good tea is always indicated by a tea pedigree name. If another one is substituted, it's not in the Good Tea class.

Tea shouldn't be eye candy, either. That is very much the feature of the mall stores that aim at capturing the peak holiday market. Whereas everyday tea drinkers aren't generally interested in artistic trappings over functional packing, when they shop for a Christmas gift, they are too ready to pay a lot more for something that looks outstandingly good. That means The Tin or The Designer Box.

The high-end stores are likely to be located in high rent malls, tourist centers and affluent customer traffic areas. They are quite different from the local ones, especially in that they are almost invariably part of a national or regional chain. Their outstanding feature is that these companies know how to put together an engaging shopping experience, have tempting and colorful accessories, and a very few offer some outstanding teas as well.

Boutiques' high fixed rental costs drive their prices. They are designed to elevate the apparent quality of their teas as superior to the average and hence worth paying extra for. You can be sure that the tea palace stores will have very high prices.

But not the best teas. They too often sell $5 an ounce good but not great ones for $10. Gourmet tea stores, kitchen and cooking boutiques routinely stock items in the $40 to $200 range. Too many use this customer expectancy about price points to add an egregious surcharge to their tea offerings. If that elegant double glass teapot costs $72.99, then the tin alongside it, a hundred grams (3.5 ounces) of pompous labeling as an – or The or Our— Imperial Blend #24

China black tea, can look attractive at $22.95, even though it's basically the same quality as an $8 supermarket blend.

Here's a *Tea Tips* recommendation: if the tin looks terrific, assume the tea is average, at best, unless you see evidence to the contrary. Even the most elegant and well-made tin costs under a dollar wholesale, including custom design and printing.

Online sellers

By far the major shift in the tea market is hardly surprising: online sellers. They have a huge advantage over physical stores in the extent of inventory that they can manage. While local tea shops are fun to browse around and pick up a few special items, their stock is generally well under 100 items in total.

If you are interested in very top end very special very different teas, you'll need to find a luxury specialist, but for any tea, including rare puehrs, Taiwan small producer oolongs and Japanese seasonal harvests, Moonlight whites and pedigree smallholder greens and oolongs, you will be able to find an outlet online regardless of where you live.

The online/store distinction – clicks or bricks –is illustrated by, say, shopping for an Adam's Peak Sri Lanka white tea. You can expect to pay $30 an ounce if you can find it (it's worth the price; this is a tea that is the embodiment of the ancient Greek myth of ambrosia, the nectar of the gods.) Good luck searching for it in a physical store. There are maybe fifty in the US stocking it. That's just a guess.

Adam's Peak is simple to locate online, and, yes, that includes on Amazon and eBay, which usually has around five very good deals. There is some peripheral fluff and misinformation: ads for Adam's Peak black tea, which is non-existent, for instance, and a few which are unclear on shipping or exact sourcing but there are typically around twenty excellent online offers to choose from, at competitive prices.

This is just one example of the transformation over the past few years in tea shopping. Keep in mind, though, the four questions for shopping: how clear are you about what you are looking for, how precise and useful is the information about the tea, what is the suppler selling: tea or packaging/presentation/up market extras, and how knowledgeable is the seller?

The online sellers range from the highly-personalized sites where the knowledge and expertise of the firm's buyers and tasters are made apparent through their descriptions and selectivity, often supported by short articles and blogs, to larger ones that use the advantages of Internet to combine focus and breadth in offering a wide variety of teas and deals, but often with only limited or cut-and-paste boiler plate ad copy.

To some degree, the primary distinction among the online sites is self-service smorgasbord versus in-store assistance. You need to be clear about one you're buying from. The portals like Amazon and eBay provide the inventory and deals and leave the information for you to assess. Amazon's list of over a hundred *thousand* teas includes low end and pedigree teas. There are many excellent buys, but a surprising amount of the information is blatantly incorrect. Its reviewers provide some assistance but even basic data is incomplete, ambiguous, missing or wrong.

Here are two essentially random examples of Darjeeling teas for purchase on Amazon. They are "eyeball" selections simply because there are 34,000 listings for Darjeelings. The search criterion was a low price and well-known brand or garden. The first result is a teabag blend, that costs just over fifteen cents a cup, and the other an estate first flush that is even less expensive and cheaper than almost any supermarket bag: $21 for a full pound, a mere 10 cents a cup. If these are good quality teas, each is a spectacular deal. But...

The first problem is that it is impossible to be sure about the grade. There are a lot of pedigree name teas listed on these sites that imply they are premium grades but turn to be less than promised. Many provide no indication at all. The tea bag blend in this example avoids any details. It can only be low level dust. The ingredients list states that it is black tea; that's it, though the marketing description talks about the brand name firm sourcing its Darjeeling leaf from the best gardens, where it is hand plucked. Yet, in the fine print, the tea is described as coming from the Darjeeling "region."

The estate tea is a first flush from a top rate garden, one of the best and oldest in Darjeeling. $21 a pound is as low as tea gets. Here's the catch. The estate's whole leaf top grade 1st flush sells for $230 a pound and its 2nd flush for $140. These are the *Amazon* prices. $21 for a whole pound?

Scouting around the site for just a few minutes focuses the picture. Both teas are broken leaf, bought from the gardens but "manufactured" and packaged in the US, whereas whole leaf Darjeelings are processed locally. Technically, the leaf is "handpicked" Orthodox harvesting; in practice, this is all the leftovers from the final stages: fragments that break off as the leaf moves through withering and rolling, bits and pieces that fall through the sieves, and odds and ends that do not pass the rigorous manual inspection that is part of the Orthodox crafting.

One of the byproducts of learning more about tea and shopping around online is that with information and confidence comes creative skinflint bargain-hunting. The online sellers are by far the best overall resource *if you know what you are looking for and how to choose among options.* You must bring your own knowledge – you don't need a lot, essentially no more than *Tea Tips* offers – to sort through the plethora of choices.

Luxury specialists

There are a few stores, mainly in major cities, that are at the very top of the retail hierarchy. They are high-priced and selective. Many of them combine food service with tea sales. This is smoked salmon sandwiches and chocolate gateau territory. The teas will generally be a narrow selection of excellent harvests of well-known pedigree teas.

Each is unique. There are a few that have landmark status, especially in Paris. London has several of those stores where you feel honored to be permitted to enter. Think of the more as an event than a shop or café.

The *Tea Tips* review of the four circles of outlets centers on two questions: what will you find if you are just looking around? And what can you discover that's new in some way? Here's a summary of the answers:

	What to expect	Pleasant surprises
Supermarket, grocery	Brands and in-house labels; mostly bags, some blends, many flavored teas	A few with tea sections; medium grade, fair quality loose leaf
Local specialty tea stores	Fairly small inventory of mostly medium grade teas	Custom selection of a regional tea: Yunnan, Japan, Taiwan Knowledgeable owner eager to offer good advice
Gourmet and mall tea stores	Goods aimed at tourists, gift buyers, occasional tea drinkers at high prices	Elegant, attractive special items Attractive ambience and inviting store layout
Online general sites	Vast range of choices, much inaccurate information, excellent deals mixed in with average quality items	Excellent specialty sellers using eBay, Amazon as their portal with corresponding shipping and payment services
Online specialty sites	Narrow range of teas and accessories Selective and well-described Reliable offers of hard to find teas	High level of expertise and information Superb quality seasonal and smallholders' harvests
Luxury stores, tea rooms	Ambience, experience Occasional outstanding teas	As much attention to the tea as the food frou frou service

Getting the most out of your tea

Equipment and accessories

One of the special accompaniments to tea is the astonishing variety of pots, tea sets, mugs, cups, storage containers, brewing aids, infusers and other functional and decorative accessories. Most are luxuries or conveniences rather than necessities, but there are a few basic ones that enhance the overall tea experience and where your choice makes a distinct difference.

For example, the material and shape of the most common accessory of all, the cup, has a substantial effect on a tea's taste. Porcelain and glass are far superior in this regard to plastics. Clay teapots have different impacts on brewing than metal ones. There are many simple double wall glass tumblers with built-in infusers that match the convenience of tea bags but provide a much better brew of any type of loose tea. Finally, the containers you store tea in are as important as the tea itself, in that how they protect it from light, air, heat and odors determines not just its freshness but many elements of its flavor.

Here is a suggested set of tea tools that offer a combination of convenience, functionality – a complicated word for useful, sensible and well-designed – simplicity and cost. Their attractive colors and designs provide an appealing invitation to just try some good tea. There are five main areas: Kettles, Pots, Cups, Travel kit and Storage. You can spend just a few dollars for any of these and there's no need to pay more. Except, of course, for sheer pleasure.

Kettles

Kettles are both the most and least important part of the home or office tool set. They are the least important in that all they do is heat water. They are the most important in that they boil water. If you want to enjoy black tea, you simply must have a way to get the water temperature up to bubbling and steaming quickly.

Hot water from the faucet fails this basic requirement. Most coffee makers are limited to 180° Fahrenheit versus the boiling point of 212°. Some drip machines operate between 195 and 205°. They generally are slower than the 1200 watt fast kettles; the extra power oomph is not needed for their brewing functions.

The main distinctions among kettles are stove top, electric, and electric with temperature control. Electric kettles are cordless or plug-in. Some are plain, simple and functional and others designer creations with modernist flair, sweeping curves and aesthetic add-ons. You can spend $150 for a designer name bird whistle tea kettle with a blue handle or $20 for a brand name, whistling kettle with a colored handle. Go sleek or antique. There's a wealth of choices.

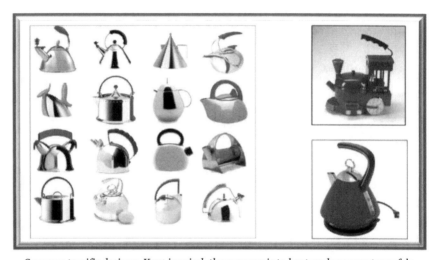

So many terrific designs. Keep in mind, the purpose is to heat and pour water safely.

Here's a checklist of what to look for in terms of the kettle doing its job: heating the water conveniently and quickly without your having to be careful that it doesn't heat, burn, scold or steam clean you:

Stove top versus electric: There is no reason to use a kettle that you heat on the electric hot plate or gas on your kitchen stove. The general preference is for electric ones. The pros of the old-fashioned kettle are that it is cheap, doesn't tie up yet another outlet and may come in nostalgic designs that recall the copper vessels whistling away on the hob. Lovers of stovetops generally like them for adding a slightly old-fashioned flavor to the rituals of tea.

Safety: A major criterion in choosing a kettle is not just is it safe for you but also for children, whether your own or visitors. Injuries from kettle accidents are rare but can be very severe. Keep in mind that you are not "heating" water the way you heat a bath but concentrating it in a small volume at the very highest temperature. Think of it as a bomb not a jug.

Look for the UL safety rating label. This will show you that the model has been rigorously tested, including for no tipping, shielded heating element, and cord protection and stability.

Make sure the lid locks tight. Check the handle is rubberized and non-slip and that the on-off switch has a power light indicator. Choose a kettle with a large lid, so that it is easy to fill and to clean inside. It's preferable that it has the standard steam whistle built in to signal it's boiling and to lessen the chance of its drying up.

Pouring: It may seem unlikely, but many kettles don't pour the water well; they are designed to look good not work most efficiently. You should be able to hold the kettle still and aim the water without wobble or awkwardness. The spout shouldn't be too long or curved; this can make it difficult to judge distance, how fast it pours and the angle of the water flow. Cordless kettles rest on a base that contains the heating element, so that when you lift them off to pour the water, they are fully free of impediment.

These cautions may sound overkill but while accidents with kettles are rare, their severity is common. Yes, these are very small risks but why take them?

Construction: The best kettles have strong seams connecting the components. The intense heat they are subject to can result in leaks. Low price steel ones rust with surprising frequency.

Plastic kettles obviously offer advantages here but cheap ones are best avoided for other than occasional use, since there is still uncertainty about the risks of both the chemical composition of the materials, their interaction with the water and their affecting its taste. The best are certified as BPA-free. BPA is a notorious and nasty compound banned in many jurisdictions as unsafe for use in baby bottles and dinnerware.

Programming: If you drink whole leaf teas that include green and oolong as well as black, it's well worth buying a kettle that provides some temperature settings. Most offer five or so, ranging from 170-212.°

The *Tea Tips* recommendation is not that you pick any particular type of kettle, only that it is worth putting a little time and thought into your choice, focusing on safety. Consumer reviews of the top buys show no pattern. Of the 10-20 highlighted in the typical list, the cost ranges from $20-70, with most towards the low end. The higher price generally reflects superior construction and attractive style, rather than better basic functionality.

Safety is the core issue. UK figures on household accidents rate hot water for coffee and tea as one of the largest causes of serious burns. The figures are high: in a population that is around 20% that of the US, there are over 100,000 serious injuries requiring hospitalization and skin grafts, plus over 300,000 others needing treatment.

Almost half the injuries are to children under five. These tend to be serious because they mostly affect the upper body, including face and eyes, *since* the little one pulls or tips the kettle or pan from above head height.

Here's the scary figure: a child exposed to hot water at just 140° for 6 seconds may need a skin graft. That is cooler than the 160° average for hot coffee and way below the 212° of a steaming kettle. Extrapolate the impact of that for 20 seconds.

As technology and materials improve, the traditional kettle is becoming a component in an integrated heater/brewer/server maker that comes ever closer to fully automating the tea making process.

Some of these are superb with simple controls to select the temperature/time combination for individual types of type and mechanisms to best handle how and when the leaf is permitted to interact with the water.

These are "modern" but the venture to enable you to get your cup of tea that brings you into the morning world of the living out from semi-narcoleptic somnambulism dates back a century. For once in the history of tea it did not emerge from the mists of Chinese antiquity but British ingenuity and tinkering. Here is the patented Teasmade device, from 1904.

1904 Teasmade: from the wonderful folk who brought you Monte Python.

The alarm clock releases a plate that strikes a match which lights the spirit stove which heats the kettle which tilts and pours the tea. SMade in China wi-fi Android Web-accessible app. But still a kettle that heats water.

Teapots

Between the kettle and the cup sits the teapot, except that tea bags don't need it. Whole leaf tea is more demanding and needs something to brew it where it can expand before being strained into the cup.

The selection of the pot that does the brewing can make it more enjoyable and actually improve it. Shape, material and porosity affect flavor, aroma, heat retention and cooling, maybe just a little but enough to add an extra silent moment of calm pleasure that is part of the tea experience.

Many tea lovers get extra pleasure from the wide range of styles, patterns, appearance and feel of their pots. The materials – clay, ceramics, iron, copper, silver and glass – have provided a vehicle for stunning and imaginative design. One book shows 2,300 British tea pots alone.

One of the favorites of experts on Chinese teas are the legendary Yixing pots. These are made of a purple clay mined only in a small town outside Shanghai. They absorb flavors to such a degree that tradition requires using them for one tea only. They store the traces of the compounds that build aroma over two years or so.

Xiying is a pottery town, with hundreds of stores; many are machine made and few use the unique zisha – "purple clay"

Yixing pots are great just to look at on a display shelf. Their provenance is difficult for the non-specialist to judge. The original red clay that makes them unique has been mined out. There is still some old zhuni clay is use by artisan potters. There's a whole town of nothing but Yixing pots and you'll find thousands for sale online, generally in the $50-100 range.

Tea Tips is very focused on the sensible: choosing quality teas over frou frou packages, focusing on the leaf not the marketing, and getting value for your money. But there's still plenty of room for personal indulgence and I-like-it buying, with no reasons needed.

Teapots in general and Yixing ones in particular are examples. They are attractive and inexpensive. It's one of the instances of "antiques" on an eBay listing not requiring a second mortgage to afford. The Xiying pots are in most instances just old. Real crafted ones with a provenance are rare.

They all look great, as do comparable old English, Japanese and Chinese ones. They add style and occasion to teatimes. A beautiful traditional soft paste mid-1800s Staffordshire porcelain pot like the one below is typically around $70 and excellent simpler ones like the glass and Amsterdam design glazed ceramic are $10-25.

Classic teapot deigns: the delicate but sturdy porcelain Staffordshire, functional glass pot, and robust household reliable Amsterdam.

You don't need anything special and exotic unless you are a drinker of very high end oolongs and puehrs, where reserving the pot for individual ones does make a difference. Many tea lovers with good palates use gongfu teapots, very small Japanese and Chinese vessels that are used to serve, say, a Dan Hong or Da Hao oolong in small servings that are quickly steeped with many infusions.

You probably don't want to deal with all this. You just need something affordable that does the job quickly and without debates on Scandinavian clay brutalism versus Japanese cast iron witch cauldrons. Increasingly, the pot is an anachronism. More and more vessels combine pot and cup.

In the days of the Brown Betty, the traditional and long-established hefty round pot that was commonplace in British homes, the kettle heated the water, the pot brewed the tea and it was then poured through a strainer into the cups.

The old mainstream of porcelain pots has been replaced by glass plus infuser as the norm

The key modern development was to put the strainer inside the pot and them inside the cup, as an infuser. A typical example is the glass tea maker with a valve. You place it on top of your cup and watch it drain. A mesh filter keeps the leaf in the tea maker. It couldn't be easier to use or to keep clean. It also enables the tea brewing showmanship trick of brewing one whose leaf expands from a dry spoonful to half a cup when wet – a Tie Guan Yin oolong or Jasmine Pearl green offers panache and terrific taste.

A flowering green tea unfolding its tied-in scarlet chrysanthemum blossom in the glass looks terrific and is not at all bitter – one of the Show and Tell object lessons. (It's also not particularly good but still much, much better than the average green in a bag.)

These tea makers sell for $20-30, depending on the material used and the elegance of the design. There is a wide range of variants on the basket/pot/cup combination. Many add portability in response to the reality that tea and coffee are very much drinks on the go. People getting ready to drive to work or catch a bus or train want to make a hot drink fast and take it with them.

Teamaker kettles and pot

If you are a whole leaf tea lover, willing to pay for something special but selective and on the lookout for bargains, there's one class of accessories that stands out in the market as unmatched. These are the equivalent of the coffee makers that can look like the control panel of a fighter plane, able to calibrate the grind, steam, category, launch speed, etc. Tea makers haven't reached that degree of automation but there are several on the market that play a similar role, with one stand out difference: gently nurturing the leaf.

Tea Tips avoids recommending or panning specific consumer brands, stores or companies, but it would be incomplete without discussing the programmable tea maker and pointing to the Breville brand.

This is by far the best way to make tea in terms of bringing out its flavors, providing maximum convenience, automatically handling the best combinations of time and temperature, and making it easy to fine-tune every element of the process.

The device has two parts: the tempered glass container with a built-in basket and a base that contains the heating element and programmable panel. As is standard for many tea makers, you can select the type of tea – black, white, herbal, etc. – and how strong you want it and the machine sets the time and temperature and automatically cuts off the brewing when it is complete, and allows for manual adjustments to fine-tune the process.

The innovation is the basket. This contains the tea and automatically lowers itself into the water when it reaches the specified temperature and lifts back up when the time is complete.

This may sound a minor detail but it transforms the brewing because the water does not hit the tea and immediately starting cooling; instead, the tea maker maintains the exact temperature throughout. It also includes controls to keep it warm and since the leaf has been removed, there is no stewing.

The Breville teamaker: the best of today and
probably obsolescent in the era of wireless software apps

The machine is expensive and there are several cheaper ones. Expect to pay around $250 for the top of the line brand and half that for others that lack a few of its features and its striking construction. Obviously, that's a significant outlay but it pays off directly in getting the maximum flavor from a tea, to the degree that it improves it by almost a grade. A low priced Nilgiri becomes a fine one. A middle range oolong has an extra subtlety and temperamental, ultrasensitive Japanese senchas can be exactly calibrated to deliver their superb smoothness and not the paint-stripper bitterness that half a minute or ten-degree difference can make.

Good tea needs a good teacup

From kettle to pot to cup... Big to little, fancy to plain, expensive to cheap. It's natural to take the cup for granted here. Generally, drinkers make no distinction between a mug or a cup, or coffee or tea use, and check what the size is, does it have a handle, is it clean and, maybe, is it dishwasher safe?

But the cup plays a surprisingly role in finishing off what the kettle starts by making sure the water is just right and the pot continues in getting the brewing exact for this individual tea. The cup adds its own interactions between leaf and water.

How many times have you made the very same tea as yesterday, in the same amount and with the same brewing time and temperature, but it's not quite as good – a little flatter, maybe, or less aromatic? You used the same tried and trusty teapot, infuser or tea maker. So, why the difference and disappointment?

Maybe it's the cup, not the tea. It's easy to treat all the coffee mugs, tumblers and tea cups you have at home or in the office as pretty much the same. Most tea drinkers don't know or care exactly what they are made of: ceramic, glass, stoneware, porcelain, plastic, earthenware, melamine, or even polystyrene, and whether it's glazed or in natural form. They mainly grab whatever is near at hand or have a cup they cherish for some aspect of its design: personalization, alma mater logo, sports team or souvenir nostalgia.

Cups are not that interchangeable. The materials they are made of have a surprising impact on tea taste, especially for an aromatic tea whose flavor offers some complexity, so it's worth being more selective.

If you want to get the best out of the tea you drink, switch your thinking from what style of cup you want to what type of material it should be made of. Very roughly, there are three overlapping elements of the tea experience: (1) the initial aroma and first sip, (2) the "mouthfeel" and full taste in the body of the tea, and (3) the aftertaste and lingering "notes" of the drink. The cup can affect any of them, sometimes dampening out what should be part of the overall pleasure.

Everyday instances are the porous clay in a standard coffee mug trapping some of the initial boost of aroma, the tea cooling too quickly and losing zip, or a hint of a plastic taste in the fresh-made brew. Less frequent or even indiscernible impacts are lead and cadmium leaching from the hard glaze that is added to the inside surface of the cup to make it less porous, and stored up water droplets blowing up the cup in the microwave. (Yes, it does happen.)

Here are the basic requirements for a cup that brings out the best in your tea. It should:

Be nonporous so that it does not interfere with the unfolding of the aromas and flavors; the material should be neutral and not "leach" – transfer molecules from the cup – or leave traces of the tea's compounds trapped in its tiny pockets of space. (Xiying pots are the reverse; their distinctive feature is to trap the flavors and let them permeate the clay over years.)

Modulate the heat of the tea to meet your preferences: keep it hot or cool it down quickly. A cup that is broad at the top cools tea more quickly than a tall, narrow one, which, however, concentrates the aroma. This is comparable to the different shape of glasses for red and white wines. Ceramic cups tend to retain heat longer than glass ones. Thinner cups transfer heat faster.

Be safe: chemically, in dishwashers and microwaves, and inert, with minimization of any interactions between the material and the tea. Borosilicate glass is excellent in this regard, but the very fact that it is highlighted in ads as "BPA-free" indicates that BPA-loaded is definitely not good. Bisphenol A (BPA) is used to harden plastics and is banned for many applications. The same applies to dishwasher safe; the term warns you that there are plenty of unsafes around.

The main choices: ceramics, glass and plastic

Tea cups are made of three main types of material: ceramics, glass and plastic, with cast iron occasionally used. These provide for a near-countless variety of shapes, sizes, decorations and features, along with differences in specific chemical compositions that affect heat transfer and porosity. They all offer wonderful designs, so you don't have to give up appearance and style for function, or the reverse. (Many of the differences among materials apply to kettles and cups, too.

You could collect tea ware by buying something new every day of your life and never exhaust the range of English-style dainty cups and saucers, Chinese porcelain, metal/glass combinations traditional in Turkish and Russian tea cultures, and tiny Japanese ones designed for ceremonies and special tastings. There are so many: Yunomi, Arita Gosho, Stafford, Winged Grace, broken loop, footed, moustache, zarf, zhong, podstakannik, kumidashi chawan...

European cups with handles, Chinese small bowls and Middle Eastern glassware.

But don't let the varied styles divert you from the core characteristic of any cup's composition: how porous is it? For general use, the less porous the better. Increasingly, too, the tougher the better; cups get a lot of handling and hard treatment, especially travel mugs and tumblers. Obviously, safety is a commonsense priority; here, the basic message is to avoid plastics, beware of the dishwasher and never get within reach of a microwave door.

Plastics

Plastics are lightweight, tough, inexpensive and brightly colored. They meet many purposes. Tea making is not one of them. The core problem is leaching. Silicates and clays are chemically inert. Plastics are formed of chains of polymers that vary in malleability, stability, reaction with other molecules and biodegradation.

Rather than review the options in detail, here are a few comments on individual types of plastic that add up to "Keep away." Yes, they are almost entirely safe, but... If the examples scare you: good.

Melamine is nice looking and cheap. It's the bright plastic dinnerware that usually comes in vivid single colors. It's a tempting buy. Please don't go near it. It's generally harm-free but reading the details of its chemistry and record of scandals in manufacturing and use across many types of product is a disconcerting exercise.

It is not exactly encouraging to learn, for instance, that melamine is created from dicyandiamide or hydrogen cyanide and the plastic resin made by adding urea and formaldehyde. Excessive heat can decompose this back to the original elements, "several of which are highly toxic." This is why you should never put a melamine cup in the dishwasher or microwave. Did you know that? Would you recognize melamine?

BPA, Bisphenol A, is a chemical that hardens plastics. It mimics the estrogen hormone. Tests of baby bottles, sippy cups and plastic storage containers not only show that BPA is a decided health hazard (The FDA declared it safe in 2008, a concern in 2010 and banned it from children's products in 2012) but that BPA-free alternatives are often worse in leaching chemicals.

The main risks include possible though not fully proven impacts on fertility, cardiovascular damage, endocrine disruption, impaired brain development and chromosomes. One of the major advertising highlights for borosilicate glass is that it is BPA-free. Again, did you know this? Would you recognize a non-BPA versus BPA-based cup?

Polystyrene foam cups: officially classified as "probably carcinogenic" by the State of California. Proven to lose a little weight when used for hot drinks. That weight goes somewhere: inside you. A striking test is to add lemon to the tea in a styrofoam cup. It melts quite nicely in boiling water.

Reusable paper cups: these are coated inside with paraffin wax and polyethylene plastic coatings and the lid is invariably plastic. This leaches into the liquid. It is a common source of gastrointestinal problems.

There is a simple rule offered by a physician for his patients who are mothers worried about the ubiquitous pre-ban use of BPA in baby bottles: "Use glass."

Forget plastics as a conscious choice. There really is no positive feature beyond their being light, cheap and unlikely to break. That leaves ceramics and glass: (1) porcelain and bone china high temperature fired clay and (2) double wall borosilicate glass.

Porcelain has been the material of global choice since around 1300, in China, and from the 1800s in Europe. (Chinese variants were being made as early as the 6th century.) It is thin, translucent and fragile. Borosilicate glass is better known by its trademark name of Pyrex. It is very tough and handles heat well. The thermal insulation tiles on the Space Shuttle were coated with it.

The main distinction between these two top choice materials is a slight difference in heat retention and a big one in the thickness of the lip of the cup that you drink from. (This is a byproduct of porosity that affects manufacturing.)

This has a subtle impact on teas, which may be summarized as SS for porcelain – Sit and Sip – and GG for glass – Glug and Go. The thinner the lip, the more you naturally let the tea glide onto your tongue. That's why a porcelain or bone china cup seems so refined. It encourages you to sit and savor the flavor of the tea. The thick material of glass and stoneware retains the heat well but it creates an autonomic reflex to take a big gulp of the tea.

This is fine for big flavor brews, especially the breakfast ones that you rely on to transform you at dawn's wretched light from narcoleptic zombie to functioning humanoid. But if you are trying out a range of mid-price teas, where you want to enjoy their individual lightness, aroma or aftertaste, choose the cup that helps you sit and sip. You'll be better able to sense the differences. The obvious best option is both/and not either/or: an SS porcelain cup for use at home and a GG glass double wall (a tumbler with built-in infuser) for travel and the office.

Porosity

The main source of differences in how cups affect tea is the porosity of the material: how much it is like Swiss cheese, with pinholes where air and water can penetrate it or pockets of empty space be formed by small mixed in extra bits and pieces, such as mineral particles in the rock clays that are the base for ceramics.

Porosity is measured in terms of the void-space fraction and is generally proportionate to the hydraulic conductivity, considering pore throat radii. Vuggy porosity is of relevance to geological poromechanics, though not to Earl Grey consumption.

(Apologies – sort of – for that flow of sciency poetizing, but it was too tempting an opportunity: to be the very first in the more than one thousand years of tea writing to associate in one sentence Earl Grey and non-fenestral touching vugs.)

Back to teacups and Swiss cheese…

Think of the poured hot liquid on the larger scale as a tidal flow. The cup is like a sea wall. If it's pitted with small holes and lumpy impurities, water gets trapped and that absorbs and dissipates the odors of the salt and seaweed. If it's marble-smooth, all these stay within the liquid as it flows. At a more microscopic level than sea waves cresting and crashing, the interaction between the inner surface of the cup and the brewed tea has a surprising impact, one that you may not directly taste but it's there as an awareness of something missing. It's flat and loses some of its "notes" and overtones.

Ceramics

Ceramics vary widely in porosity. The term technically means made of clay that is fired in kilns, but it is loosely used to refer to "pottery": stoneware, earthenware, porcelain or terra cotta. The clay and firing heat determine a ceramic's type. Clay is fine-grained natural rock or soil material with minerals and traces of metal oxides and organic matter.

There are many classes of clay. For cups, the main categories are:

Earthenware, the most common and easiest to work with. It hardens at a firing temperature of 950-1100 Centigrade. These are the big, intendedly clunky, pottery mugs: very porous and rough, chalky and grainy in surface. They are generally not glazed, which is the addition of a vitreous –

glass-like – coating that eliminates porosity and adds color and design. To retain heat, they are made thick in their walls.

Stoneware: 1160-1300 degrees, impermeable, dense and hard. There is a wide range of clay quality in terms of size of particles, impurities and added mica and quartz.

Stoneware may be fired once or twice, to facilitate glazing. It is heavy and thick and widely used for coffee mugs. It is inexpensive to make. It retains heat well but that means that it can crack when subjected to extremes of temperature.

This is cheap everyday functional drinkware and there is often corner-cutting in production to keep costs low. For instance, glazes may not join well to the clay and crack, forming "crazy" spider web-like patterns.

When this happens, throw the cup away. Immediately. even tiny cracks can provide nesting hideaways for bacteria. Never use a dishwasher no matter what the manufacturer states about this being safe; stoneware is rigid and intolerant of heat changes.

All in all, stoneware is acceptable but not outstanding on any dimension of cup features, including variety of shape. Most tea cups and coffee mugs are uniformly cylindrical, with the bottom and lip being pretty much the same radius. Its structural characteristics mean that they are invariably thick-lipped Glug and Go.

A small but definite concern about stoneware in particular and ceramics in general is that many of the most popular glazes get their brightness and color from lead and cadmium oxide. This "by the way" comment by an expert is a little disconcerting: "The toxicology of ceramic materials is often underestimated and sometimes neglected in our ceramics institutions." He describes the consequences of cadmium exposure as gruesome and, it seems, not infrequent.

Another analysis states that "there are some glazes that contain lead and cadmium and still say that they are dinnerware safe..." and "a small amount of leaching is allowed by law." It makes the point that no one can know what will happen to a glaze after years of the cup being used, run through the dishwasher thirty or more times, the glazes having "crazed", and they have been microwaved who knows when. "Some potters say that you should never use these ingredients for dinnerware. Never, period."

Porcelain: typically fired at 2300 degrees but this may be reduced to 1900 by adding mineral ingredients. Uses clay with very fine particles, mainly kaolin, also known as china clay. It is hard to work with because it lacks the plasticity and malleability of the clays used in earthenware and stoneware. Cracks and deforms easily in firing since the ideal density is achieved very close to the melting point.

The result is a thin, almost translucent, delicate and smooth cup. It doesn't need glazing to ensure nonporosity, though light glazes are often added for decoration. Variants use "hard paste" clay mixed with feldspar, kaolin and quartz and marks German Meissen porcelain.

Soft paste adds soapstone, lime and what is termed "frit" mixtures of enamels, minerals and other clays. It was the breakthrough development in matching Chinese porcelain and produces a more granular and shiny white body than hard paste, with the advantage of lower firing requirements. French Sevre china is a noted example.

Bone china is technically different from porcelain and fine china, but has the same characteristics. It's more fragile but cheaper to make. It adds bone ash to the clay, from cow bones, a creepy idea for some people. It was invented by Spode and became the dominant material used in English tea ware.

Porcelain and bone china are terrific choices for cups, except for their fragility. They look good, are a pleasure to handle and keep tea warm. They do not interfere with the flavor or leach. Porcelain remains the choice of professional tea tasters. It has historically been accompanied by the saucer, and that remains the case for the traditional tea set, which has smaller cups that are narrow at the bottom and widen out to the top. High tea ceremonies invariably include saucers. Tea drinking as everyday routine doesn't need them.

Glass

Glass is a classic material for both teapots and cups: nonporous and very smooth. It is commonplace in Russia, Turkey and Morocco, using standard breakable glass made of lime soda. The Russian podstakannik is typical: an ornate metal basket into which the tea glass fits and is protected.

The more popular, practical and portable option is tough borosilicate glass. This adds boric oxide to the standard silicate ingredients, making it resistant to extreme temperatures and chemical corrosion. If it breaks, it doesn't shatter into pieces but cracks, snaps and collapses. It's more expensive to make than lime-soda glass, which is widely used in kitchenware, including glasses for cold drinks.

The old: Russian podstakannick glass   The new: double-wall borosilicate

Old and new: borosilicate handles heat and cooling well, doesn't need protective holder

Tea cups that use the glass are increasingly double-walled: a cup within a cup. The outer and inner pieces are blown separately, dried and firmed up, and then joined together. The inner one keeps the tea hot while the outer one ensures the cup is cool to the touch. Glass does not require glazing and is easy to keep clean, with no need to use the dishwasher.

There's not much to add about borosilicate. It is an excellent choice for everyday use, equal to but less fragile than porcelain. You really can't go wrong in picking it.

How the cup handles heat is one of the last but very important criteria in picking the best type of cup for yourself. You sometimes want the tea to cool quickly or sometimes stay hot, depending on the situation. You also would prefer that the one piece of tea ware that you put in the dishwasher emerges as still one piece and is not cracked, smushed or melted.

Your choice here will center on shape rather than just material. The best combination is porcelain/bone china with a wide lip radius for cooling, and cylinder-shaped tall and narrow borosilicate glass with a double wall to keep the tea hot. Then sit back and enjoy tour tea at its best and at your leisure.

Lessons from a road warrior

There's a critical element missing in the accessory list: the Road Warrior tool kit. At home, you have access to all you need. You can be sure of getting hot water, you choose your whole leaf tea from the tins in your cupboard, bring out that lovely china tea set.

It's not quite the same on the road, whether you're in a hotel palace in Rio, a conference center in Tokyo, an airport motel of indeterminate location and quality, a training center with a stand-up buffet breakfast table, or an office with a coffee machine and cupboard of powdered milk, polystyrene cups and those tea bags of indeterminate age, quality and origin.

Face it. You can't expect to find good tea easily, if anywhere, on trips away from home, and hot water is a contradiction in terms globally. So, Warrior, arm yourself. You need to take with you some basic accessories that are compact, convenient and simple. You face three challenges. The first is the water, the second knowledgeable service, and the third the unpredictability of what tea you will get.

The Challenge: Water and service. The Road Warrior response: Bring your own heater. Coffee is king in restaurants, not just because it is by far the most ordered drink but because it is easy to set up. There are plenty of published surveys and interviews with managers and staff that make it very clear that tea is a nuisance for them. Few either know or care about its special needs.

When was this poured? How old is the bag? Why the lime?!!!? How soon will it get cold? What's in the bag?

This coffee machine doesn't boil the water. The carafes are used for water and tea. The tea bags will get stewed.

Why compromise and tolerate the lack of accessories
for office, hotel, car and general waiting-around places?

Their water source is the shared coffee heater, which maintains a temperature of, typically 200°F. The staff keep the coffee pots full and move around serving and topping up customers. Tea demands a special range of temperatures for blacks, greens, etc. The server offers just "hot" water from pots that have at least traces of coffee odors that tea absorbs quickly and easily and may have cooled to as low as the 130 degrees many coffee drinkers prefer.

Travel with your own heater. Bring it into the breakfast room or office meeting if you can or brew your own tea and carry the mug in. Don't even bother trying to use the coffee maker in your room to heat water that you pour onto the tea bags provided. At best, you will get a tepid dribble. Above all, do not risk the water on a plane. Ever. Surveys consistently show that only about one in eight of the heaters are cleaned even once a month and all are breeding grounds for a truly disgusting petri dish of bacteria.

The best heaters are the small cordless plastic kettles that fit onto a base plate with a fast heating element. They generally have an 8-cup capacity, which makes them larger than the Lone Warrior needs. You'll need a soft briefcase-type attaché bag if you want to carry yours into a conference or office.

It's best to avoid the immersion coil heaters that fit into the cup. They show a high failure rate, lack the oomph to get the tea really hot and have a very short cord length. You can generally find an outlet for your heater close at hand and out of sight.

Challenge: The best container. Response: Buy a tall tumbler and small infuser. Always have your own cup/mug close at hand. The best choice is the tumbler that you'll see taxi drivers in China carrying in their car through the day. It's made of a strong ceramic or double-walled glass that helps keep the tea warm.

You need an infuser. There are many of these, ranging from disposable tea pouches – a do it yourself tea bag – to metal baskets that fit into the cup, tea balls, spoon shaped tea holders, and strainers. If you have the space in whatever you carry with you, the valve infuser is by far the best choice. It's very efficient and keeps the leaf out of the cup. Size is the only drawback; it's about 1½ times the size of a tea cup.

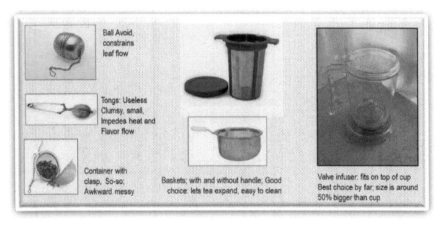

Infusers: left-hand column, poor choice, middle good, right-hand excellent

Some advice: Go beyond KISS – keep it simple, stupid – to KISSSNM – simple, small, spacious, nonmetallic. Tea balls constrain the space for the tea to expand; non-simple dangling hooks, lids, handles and big strainers don't improve the tea and make the infuser more cumbersome. The best overall small sized choice is a wire mesh basket that rests the top of the cup.

Challenge: The tea. Response. Bring your own, selected for travelling. You can never count on the tea being fresh and select even in the hotel that makes everything elegant. You must bring your own but need to pick ones that suit travel not home preferences.

Tea is a high margin item for a restaurant. It can charge $2-3 for a standard branded bag and just pour water on it. But it's low volume. Tea drinkers expect choice, so there will generally be a quasi-wooden box holding the usual range of bags: breakfast teas, lots of flavored ones, and a mix of herbal teas. It will be stale.

Not, may be but will be. Here's a figure that isn't generally discussed concerning tea bags: their expiration date. Only a few brands on the grocery and supermarket shelves show "best used by..." and then almost always on the transparent wrapping. The average is two years. Most of the typical restaurant's stock will be replenished on an ad hoc basis. Many will not have any airtight envelope and the box will be stored on a shelf.

Here are a few suggestions. They are only that and there are plenty of other options. The main point is very simple. The convenience of teabags comes their being in sealed bags; that's all. So, carry a variety of around six loose leaf teas in ziplock sandwich bags, small tins or jars with very tight lids.

The lid is key, for commonsense reasons of avoiding spillage and to keep the flavors locked in. Glass is dreadful for long term storage since light is one of its prime spoilers but for a short trip, it's fine. it's easy to get hold of baby food space saver size jars that hold up to eight spoonfuls of leaf.

For blacks, it's advisable to avoid ones that are susceptible to the attack of the bitters, because you generally don't have the same control, time and freedom to pay attention as at home. Misjudging the brewing of Ceylons and Assams can be like swallowing a jolt of polyurethane wood stain.

Nilgiri is a preferred choice. It's an undervalued tea. Nepalese teas are excellent in quality and price. These teas hold their flavor well and are tolerant of temperature and time variations in brewing. The advice for all your teas is to bring ones that are a little bit peppy so you avoid the bland and the flat that comes from often having to improvise and rush.

White teas are surprisingly good in this regard, though pricy but half an ounce won't hurt your finances and will improve your day. The ideal is a few cupfuls – maybe four teaspoons – of a Silver Needle. White teas are a better general choice than green ones unless you are sure of access to good water. There's always a tricky aspect to making them on the fly; they easily end up too bland or too bitter. So much can go wrong in the brewing and they get cold quicker than blacks and oolongs.

Oolongs are robust and reliable. Bring several, to match your mood and that state of your taste buds and heed for a little wake up or soothing: a bold Tie Guan Yin, preferably from Taiwan, a jasmine oolong and, if you can locate them, any vacuum-packed 5, 8 or 10 gram Wuyi or Alishan.

The "if" is substantial. These advanced tea bag equivalents are standard in Asian supermarkets but not in US and European tea catalogs. They are routine for oolongs. One of the most attractive of the online deals are mixes of China high end teas. This gives you a chance to try out ones that you are unlikely to see in stores.

Slightly larger than a tea bag; vacuum packing seals in freshness;
whole leaf, typically 8 grams (2 cups); open and brew

Your own Road Warrior choices may be completely different from all these suggestions. The main *Tea Tips* advice is simple: make them. If you love tea there's no reason to give up the pleasures it provides. Travelling involves compromise after compromise unless you take the offensive. The alternative is abject surrender, bowing your head and numbing your taste buds to yet another wretched Earl Grey in a Styrofoam cup of lukewarm water in the lobby of some Motel 5¼.

Storage: the freshness imperative

The last component of the tea drinker's equipment is simple, essential and too often overlooked: storage tins. The characteristics that make tea an adaptive base for fresh aromatic flavorings makes it just as responsive to kitchen odors, light, moisture and heat. It may look inert but remains chemically active and dynamic.

These attractive tins are highly functional: neutral metal lining, close fitting dual lids, plastic to close off and long lid to seal

Keeping your tea fresh and unaffected by all these external intrusions requires tins that have a very tight lid or lids kept in a place that is at a constant room temperature. They should not be opened too frequently since that allows air and damp to get to work immediately. It's that simple.

Tins can be a little expensive but there are so many beautiful designs that it is tempting to put out $15-20 or so for an attractive set of four or broadcast a few hints around birthday time.

For really fine and pernickety teas, it's a good idea to keep the tins fairly full; this cuts down on air sealed inside the tin. Two ounce ones are often the ideal choice. This may seem a minor issue but green teas, especially Japanese ones, do not keep as fresh as black and fuller oolongs, which have been more oxidated, meaning that they do not interact with air.

Increasingly, sellers are paying more attention to making sure that your tea is fresh when you buy it. Vacuum packing is becoming standard along with stand-up pouches that are coated with laminated film and zipseals. These can be resealed. They also meet one of the industry's major priorities, which is to make their products stand out on the shelf. Loose tea obviously can't be prepackaged in this way and the most common options are compostable paper bags with a tin tie.

It's tempting to keep your tea in these original packages but that tends to be a convenience that doesn't ensure maximum protection. It is easy for flavors to evaporate since the seal is not kept entirely tight. Air is the enemy. So, stick with tins.

One aspect of this wide range of accessories is that they are fun, to buy and use and even look at. Tea has been so central to so many societies for so long that it has built a tradition of superb design and craftsmanship. So many accessories add an affordable pleasure to the simple experience of making and drinking your tea. A bone china cup, double wall glass traveling tumbler, bright set of storage tins, shiny space age steel kettle... Beats a microwave, polystyrene cup and box of tea bags.

Some ending thoughts

Of necessity, *Tea Tips* has been selective in its coverage of topics. The aim has been to give you a reliable navigation map at a level of enough detail to offer clear descriptions and practical suggestions but without overloading the book with too much minutiae and sidetracks.

That means downplaying – perhaps even short-changing – some areas of potential interest and relevance to your tea choices and enjoyment. In particular, *Tea Tips* has little to say about flavored and blended teas. That's because they are very much an individual appeal, with few commonalities.

The tea is usually subordinate to the flavoring. There are some excellent brands that blend very fresh and often exotic flowers, fruit, herbs and spices that vary from the subtle to the blatant, and from natural natural to technically natural to definitely synthetic. Many of them will be herbal and not contain any true tea. The only useful comments to make about this type of drink is: Enjoy.

But be aware of the wider issues of the risks of herbal teas, the nonsensical hype about green tea as medical magic, or the tap dance evasions about just what natural and organic mean. Look both for freshness, tightly sealed packaging and, where you can, information about where the petals and pieces come from. Chamomile, for instance, varies as much in wholeness, broken and dust fragments as tea does. Egyptian chamomile is generally rated the best.

Given that the tea is just a base, an outstanding flavored tea must have an outstanding flavoring agent. It makes a substantial difference in an Earl Grey's taste and quality if the citrus is real bergamot from Sicily or machine processed dried farm crop. Complaints about disappointing jasmine teas often reflect the petals: much of the best China ones use jasmine from Tamil Nadu in Southern India. Others are made with Arabic jasmine, which comes from the Philippines. The two are very different in intensity and fragrance.

An extreme example of the difference the flavorings make is Kunlun Mountain snow chrysanthemum. It is sublime. The flower grows only in this remote and harsh region and is packed with amino acids and proteins. It's unusual in being a high mountain flower – at

10,000 feet of elevation. The yellow daisy-like bloom is wild and picked once a year, early in the morning when the sun is rising. It's then dried.

Mountain blooms: Kunlun snow chrysanthemum.

This is an herbal tea that has the body and richness of a good black tea but with an added light aroma and sweetness. The flower makes all the difference.

The *Tea Tips* suggestion for flavored teas is simply don't settle for the second-rate and pungent. Many of these are designed to sell themselves through their powerful immediate fragrance when the storage tin is opened. It's a jolt that may or may not correspond to the taste of the brewed drink.

Flavored teas are one form of blend. The mainstream is teas like English Breakfast, which is never leaf from just one source, Tea blending is well established in the British tea selling heritage. It's not part of Asian tradition. That's because black teas blend well with other blacks and green teas don't mix well at all. Leaf size must be balanced in the blend, not for aesthetic reasons but because a small leaf releases its flavor more quickly that a broadleaf one and a green one requires a different temperature than a black leaf. Both types absorb flavors easily; it's one of the distinguishing features of tea, in contrast to, say, coffee.

Blending a good tea is a matter of pairing, rather than mixing. The aim here is not to homogenize the combination of ingredients but to choose ones that bring some individual characteristic that remains apparent but is balanced with the others. For instance, a superior

English Breakfast may start with a rich China Keemun and add some cheaper Kenya leaf that gives it a fuller color and deepens the flavor. Some brisk Ceylon finishes it off. Another may be based on a strong Assam that needs softening with an extra Indonesian or African tea.

The main problem with blends is that the good ones are expensive to produce but can't command a premium price comparable to an equivalent whole leaf pedigree tea. They end up being a compromise: so-so ingredients at a good cost. That often means CTC and broken leaf.

The CTC/Orthodox choice drives all the later processing steps. It is also the point where too much marketing sleight of hand begins. Agribusiness packagers can evade the question of how good is the leaf just by putting a name on the result; the Assam and Kenya broken leaf becomes, say, Imperial Morning Blend #12. Anonymous average ingredients then are touted as a nonaverage blend of fine teas, natural tea, and sometimes an "exclusive" tea.

The most reliable blends are whole broken leaf of a good well-made Artisan variety: Darjeelings are a prime example. The final suggestion in *Tea Tips* is a slight downer: buy blends only as a cheap extra where you spot a bargain. They too often are a compromise, averaging and flattening the differences that make teas so varied and intriguing, Stick with the best.

Maybe that's the overall message. *It's all about the leaf.*

Index

About the author

Peter Keen is the author of over thirty books, mostly on business and information technology. *Tea Tips* is his second on tea, which has been a long avocation. He writes on the subject regularly for online publications.

As a professor he has served on the faculties of Harvard, MIT and Stanford and at leading universities in Singapore, Mexico, The Netherlands and Sweden. His consulting and public speaking span over sixty countries.

Peter lives in Virginia where he combines academic and consulting work and writes on tea. While, of of course, "testing it."

Printed in Great Britain
by Amazon